A COUNTRY PIANO CHRISTMAS

DEVAN ARCHER

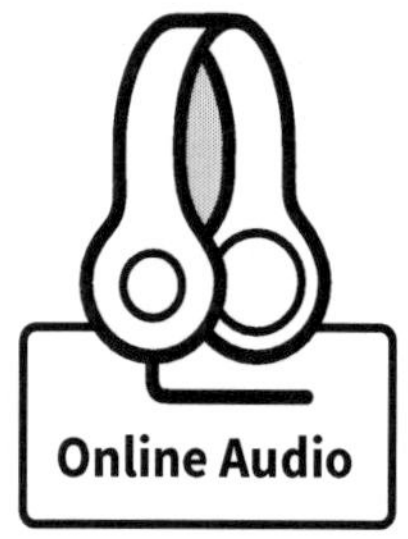

To access the online computer-generated recording go to:
WWW.MELBAY.COM/31050MEB

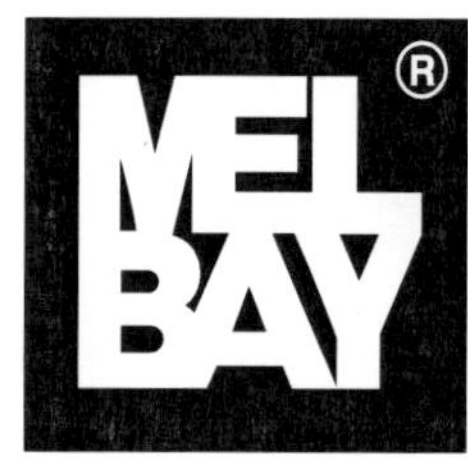

WWW.MELBAY.COM

Preface

The impact of folk songs on American society and American musical tastes has been significant since the days when such tunes were passed down from generation to generation without the aid of musical notation or formal arrangements. Over the years the elements of mountain music, western songs, railroad songs, and what has been called "early country music" have merged into a style of playing that has become very appealing and popular with almost everyone. Jazz aficionados, pop performers, folk fans, sophisticated urbanites, rural farmers, admirers of classical music, senior citizens, teenagers, kids, and almost everyone in between seems to have a favorite country tune.

Among the most popular of these songs are many of the gospel favorites that have been so widely appreciated by thousands of people. While there have been a good number of piano books published that have featured this style of playing, very little has been done in applying country keyboard techniques to seasonal pieces, especially Christmas songs. It is with this idea in mind that I have arranged this collection so that people who enjoy Christmas songs (and who doesn't?) can present them in an appealing and popular style. With some consistent practice and analysis of their application, most of the techniques herein can be applied to many other tunes.

I have made it a point to include the first two Christmas carols I learned as a small child and that still stir my heart today- "Silent Night" and "Away in a Manager." Another highlight of this book is "Jesus Came Long Ago" which is a new musical setting of "Brahms' Lullaby". I'm sure that several of your favorite Christmas songs are among those included in this collection. It is my hope that this book will bring a lot of joy to its users and listeners alike, and that it will be a significant contribution toward the development of the country gospel style of keyboard playing.

Devan Archer

Contents

As with Gladness Men of Old

1

WILLIAM C. DIX

C. KOCHER
Arr. Devan M. Archer

moderato ♩ = 60

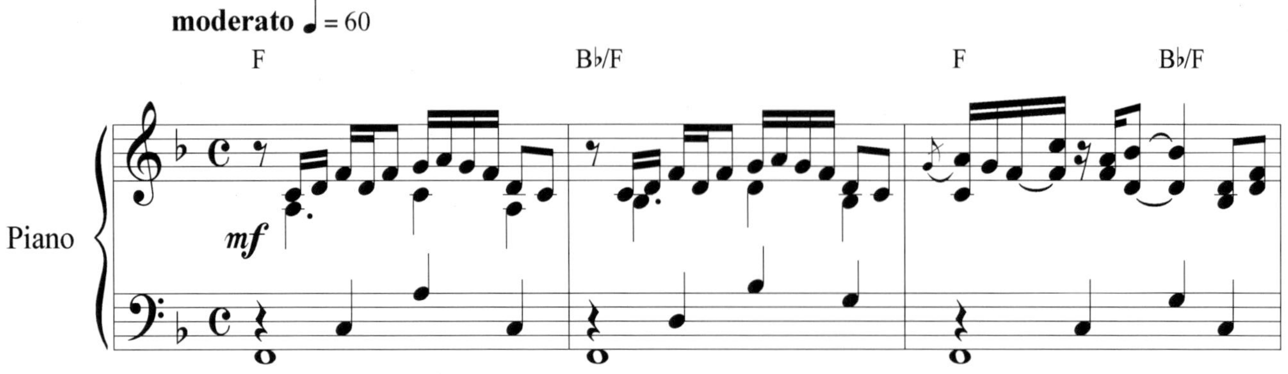

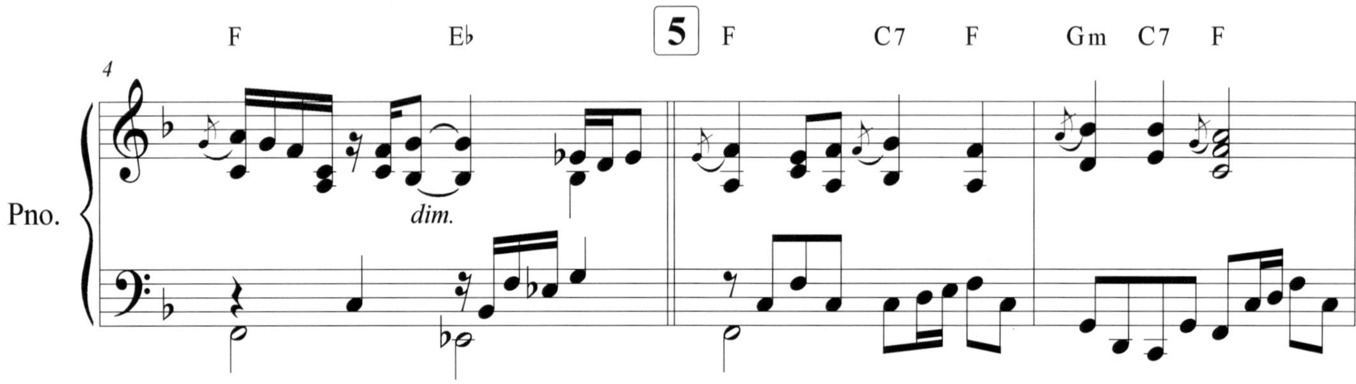

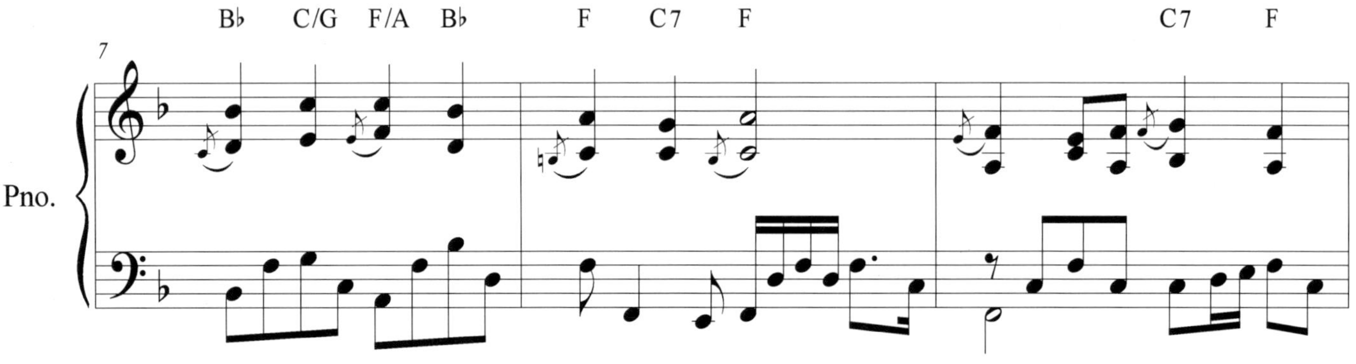

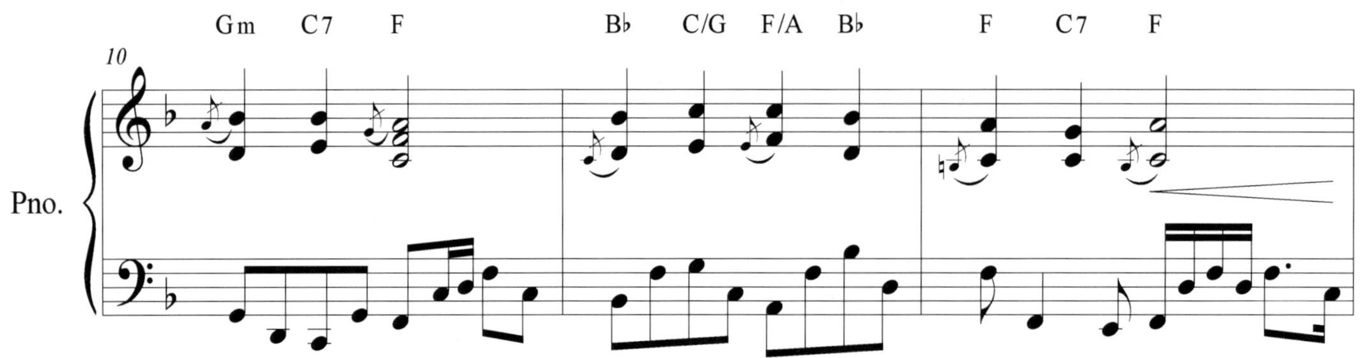

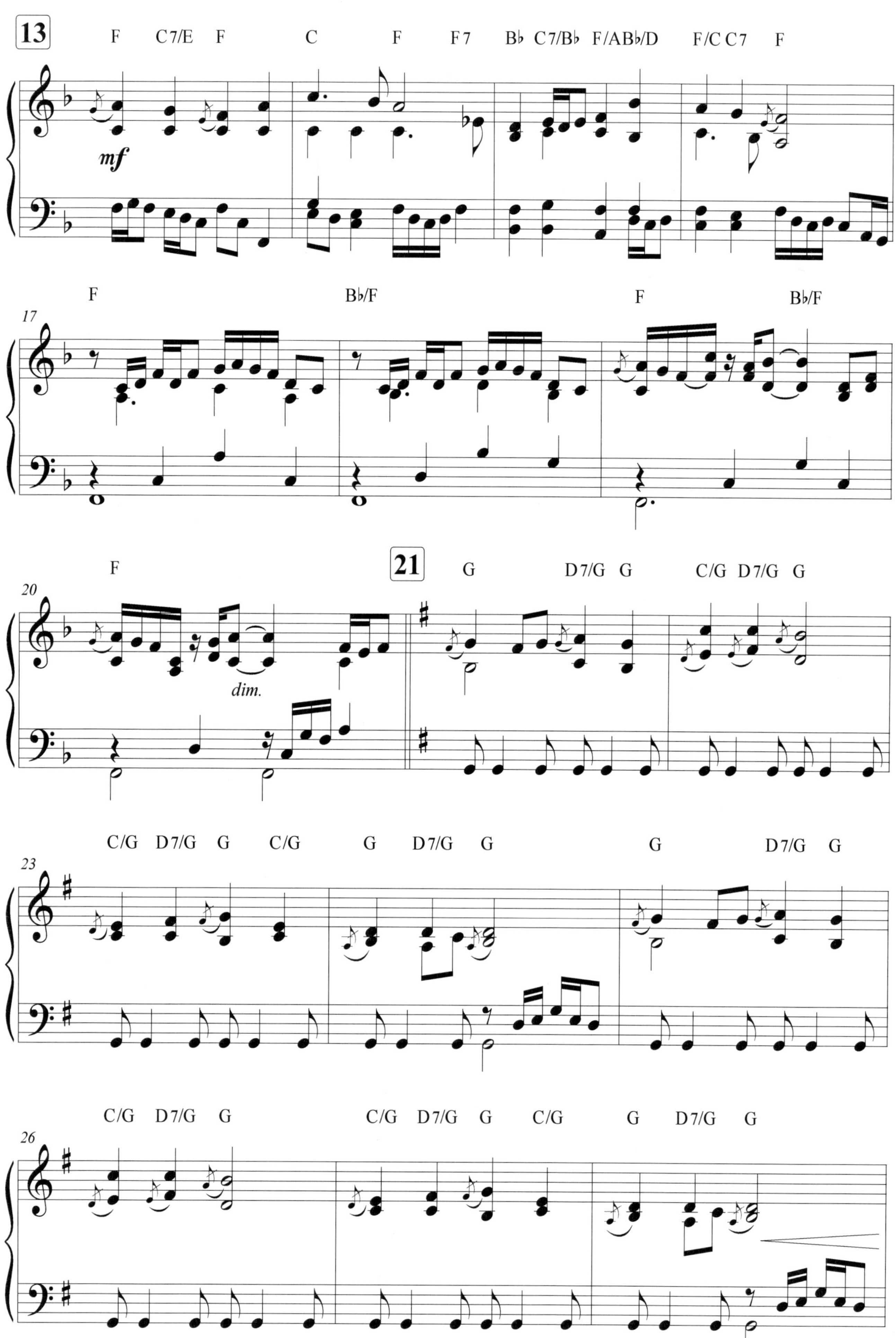
13
F C7/E F C F F7 B♭ C7/B♭ F/A B♭/D F/C C7 F
mf
17
F B♭/F F B♭/F
20
F
dim.
21
G D7/G G C/G D7/G G
23
C/G D7/G G C/G G D7/G G G D7/G G
26
C/G D7/G G C/G D7/G G C/G G D7/G G

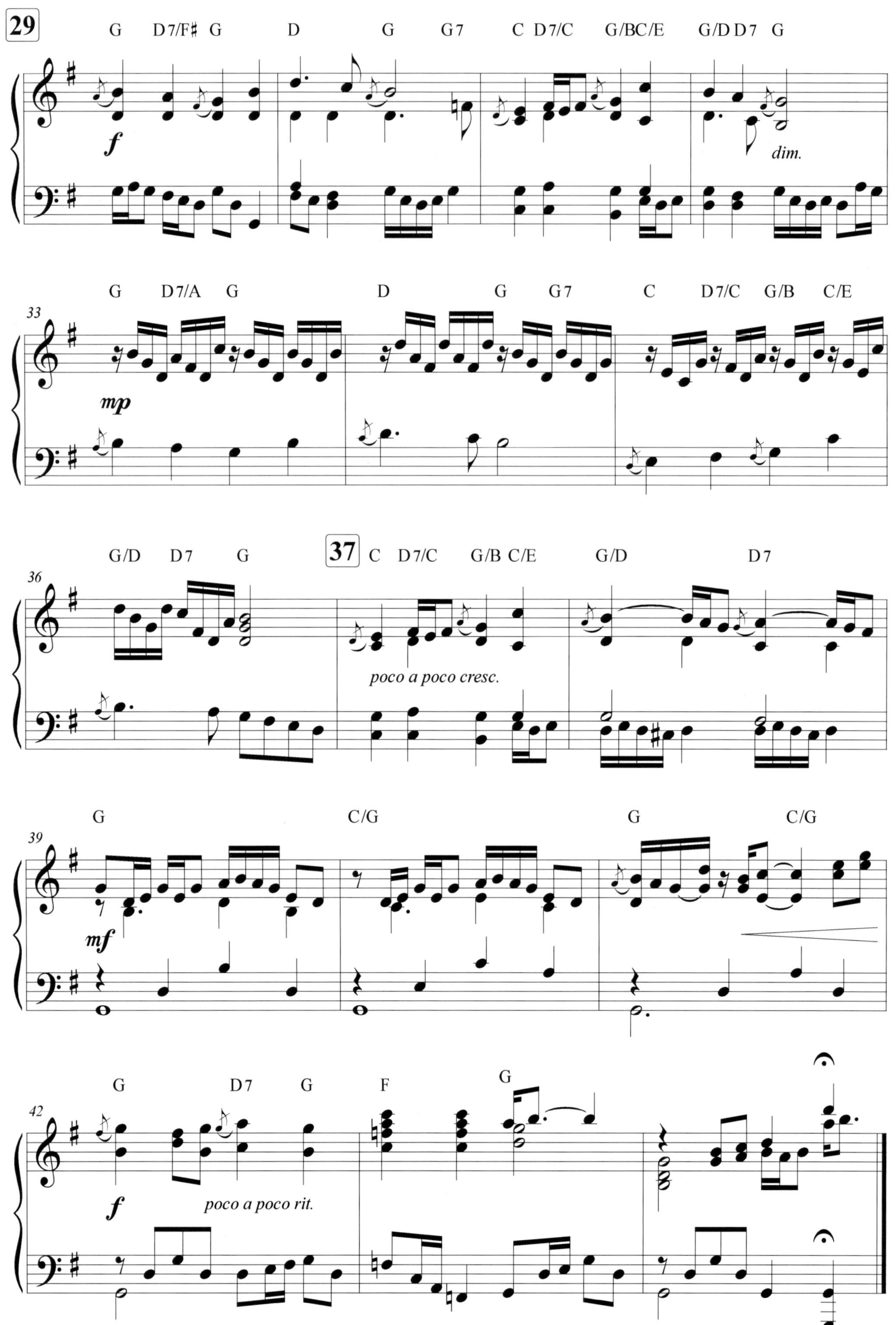
29
G D7/F♯ G D G G7 C D7/C G/BC/E G/D D7 G
f
dim.
G D7/A G D G G7 C D7/C G/B C/E
33
mp
G/D D7 G
37
C D7/C G/B C/E G/D D7
36
poco a poco cresc.
G C/G G C/G
39
mf
G D7 G F G
42
f
poco a poco rit.

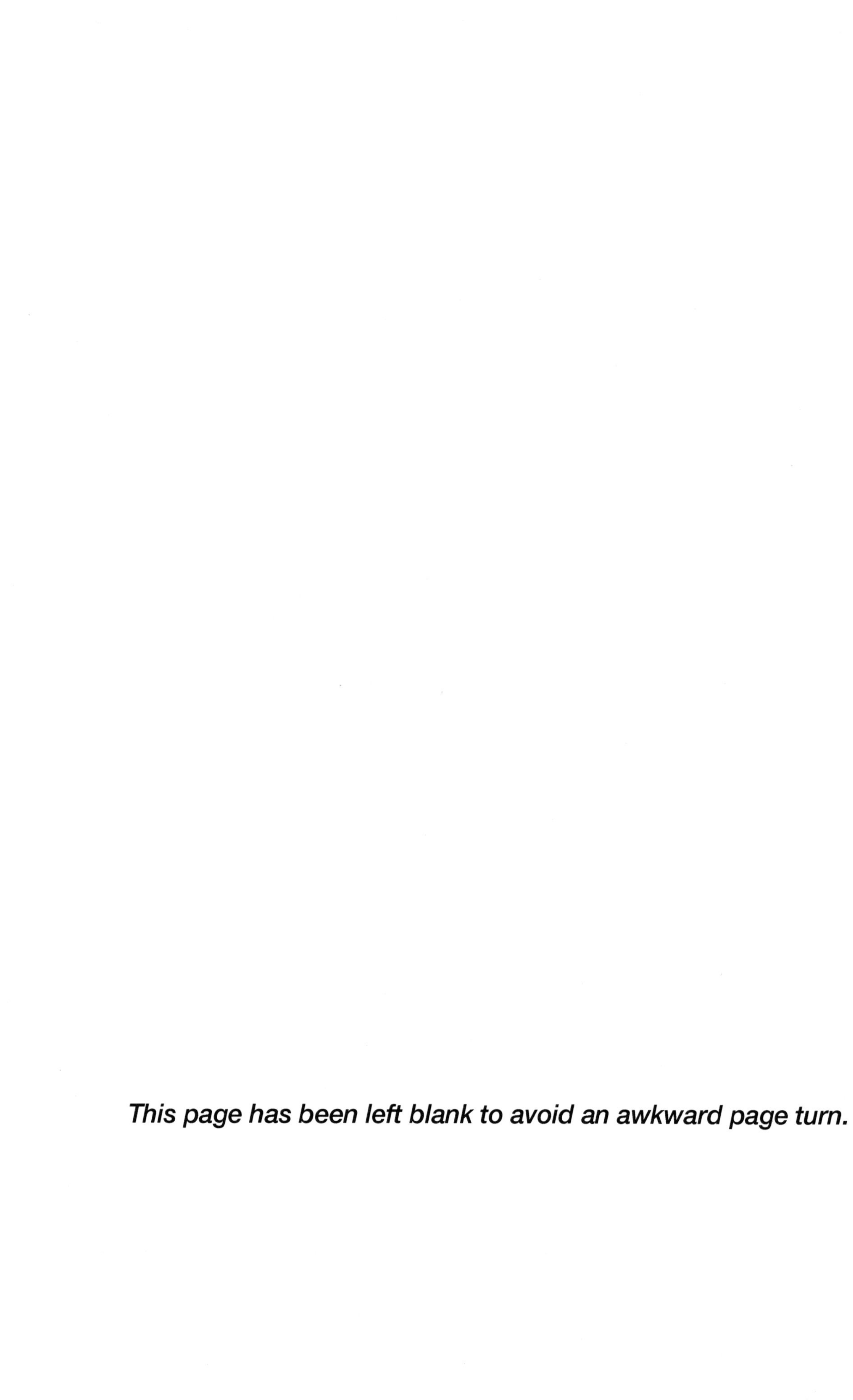

This page has been left blank to avoid an awkward page turn.

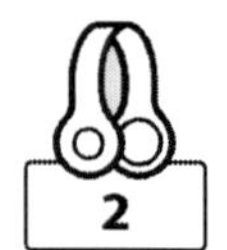

Away in a Manger

ANONYMOUS

JAMES R. MURRAY
Arr. Devan M. Archer

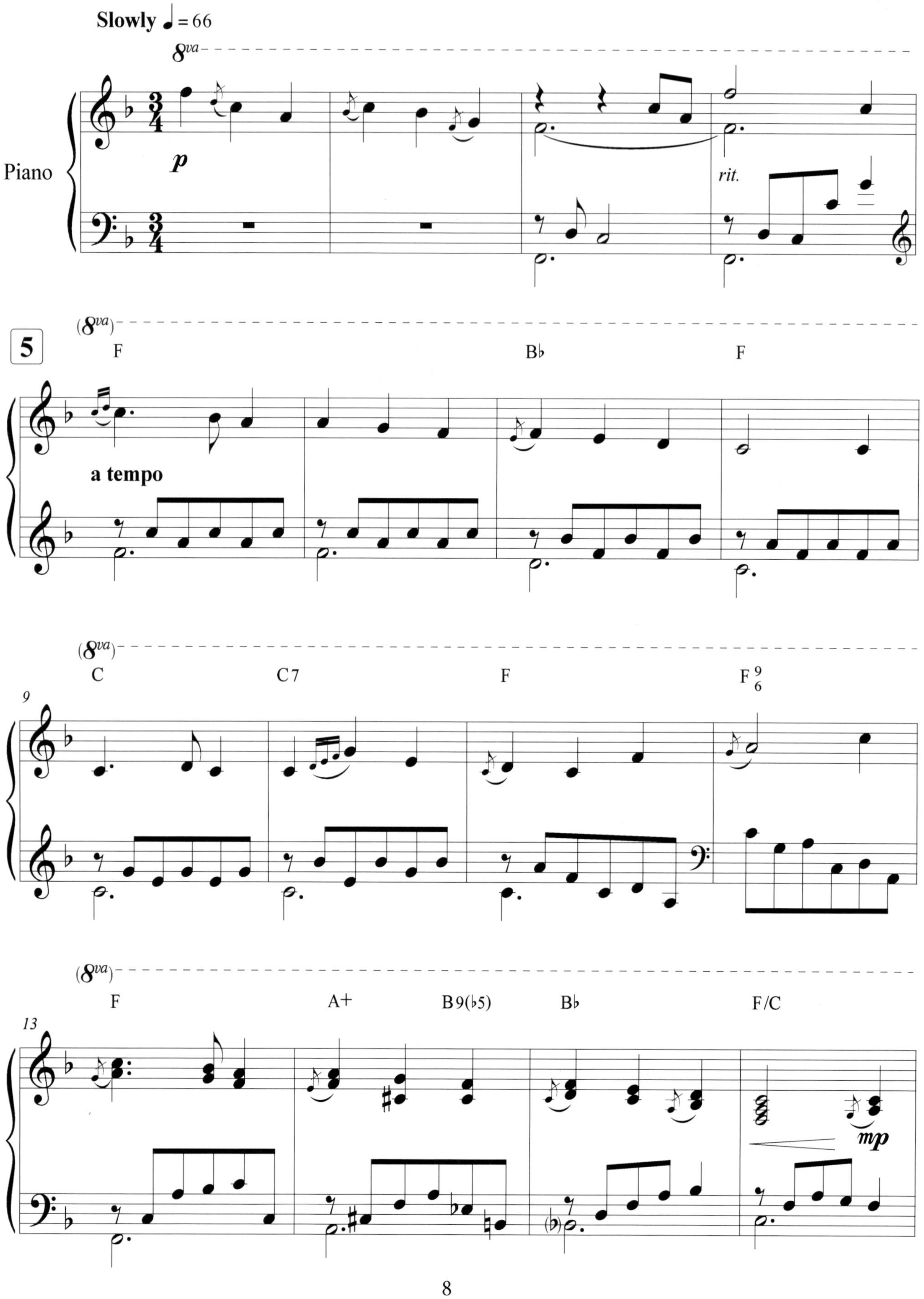

Slowly ♩ = 66

8va

Piano

p

rit.

5

(8va)

F B♭ F

a tempo

9

(8va)

C C7 F F 9/6

13

(8va)

F A+ B9(♭5) B♭ F/C

mp

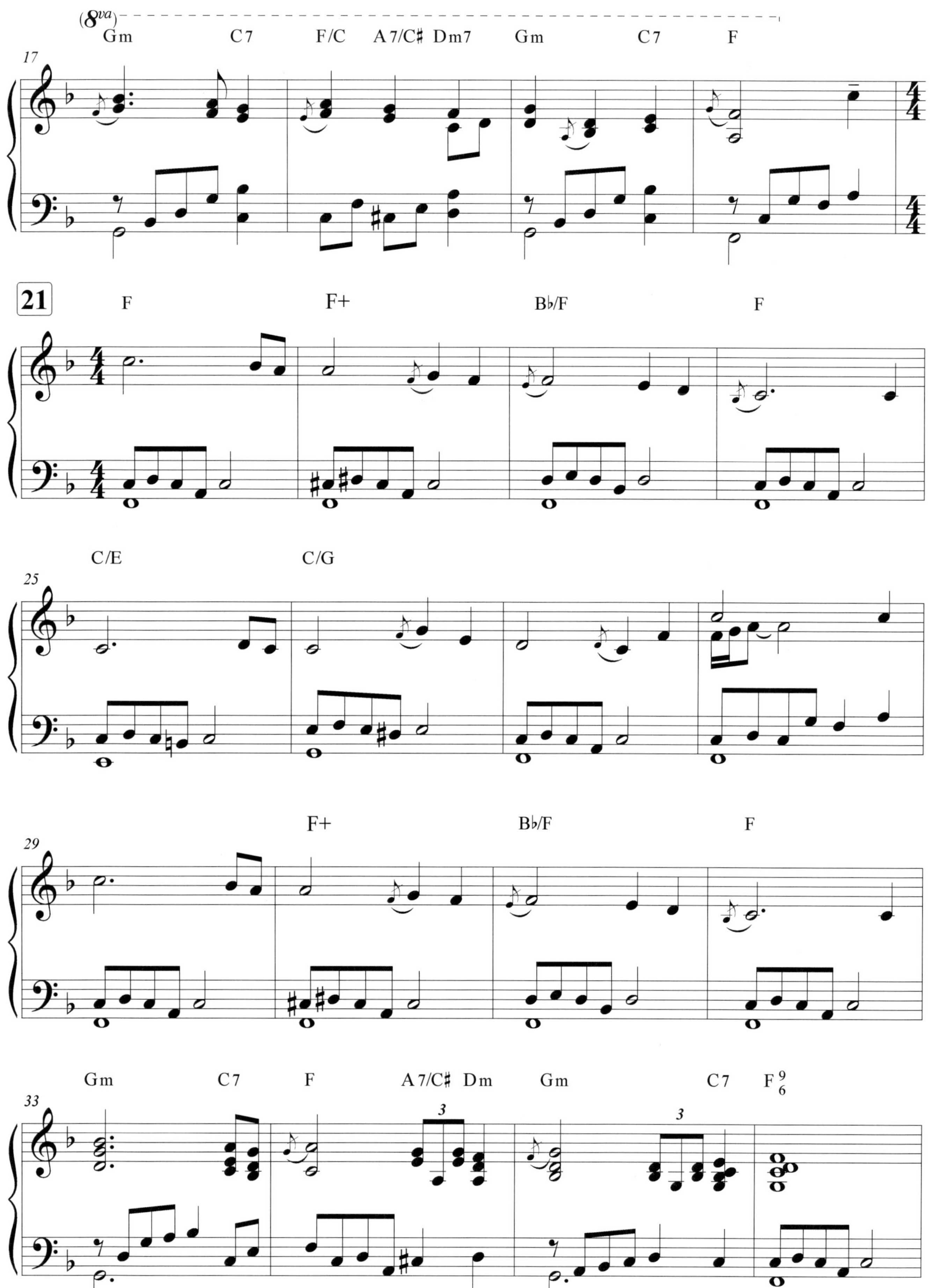
(8va)
Gm C7 F/C A7/C♯ Dm7 Gm C7 F
17
21
F F+ B♭/F F
C/E C/G
25
29
F+ B♭/F F
Gm C7 F A7/C♯ Dm Gm C7 F 9 6
33
3
3

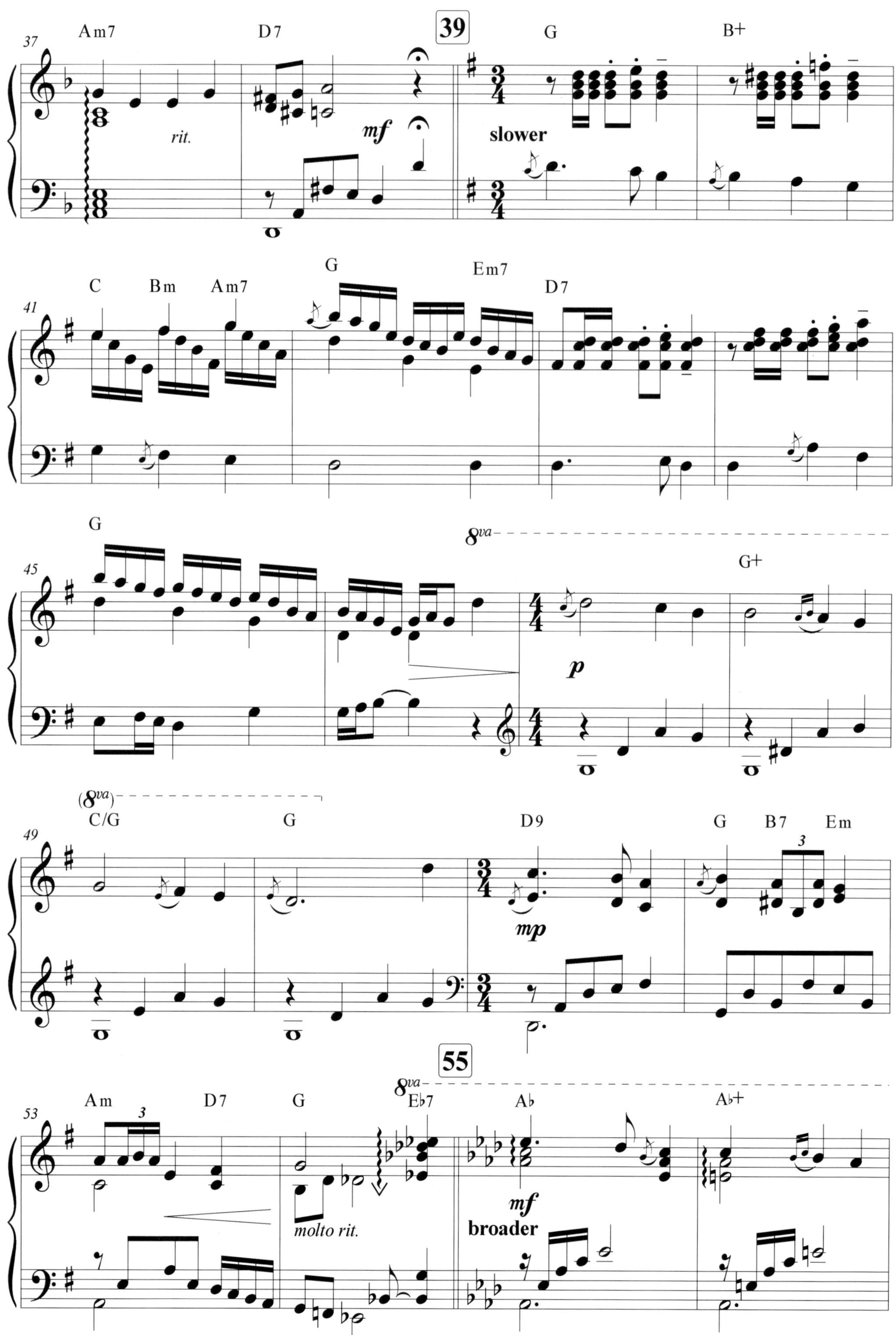
37
Am7
D7
rit.
mf
39
G
B+
slower
41
C
Bm
Am7
G
Em7
D7
45
G
8va
G+
p
(8va)
49
C/G
G
D9
G
B7
Em
mp
55
53
Am
D7
G
8va
E♭7
A♭
A♭+
molto rit.
mf
broader

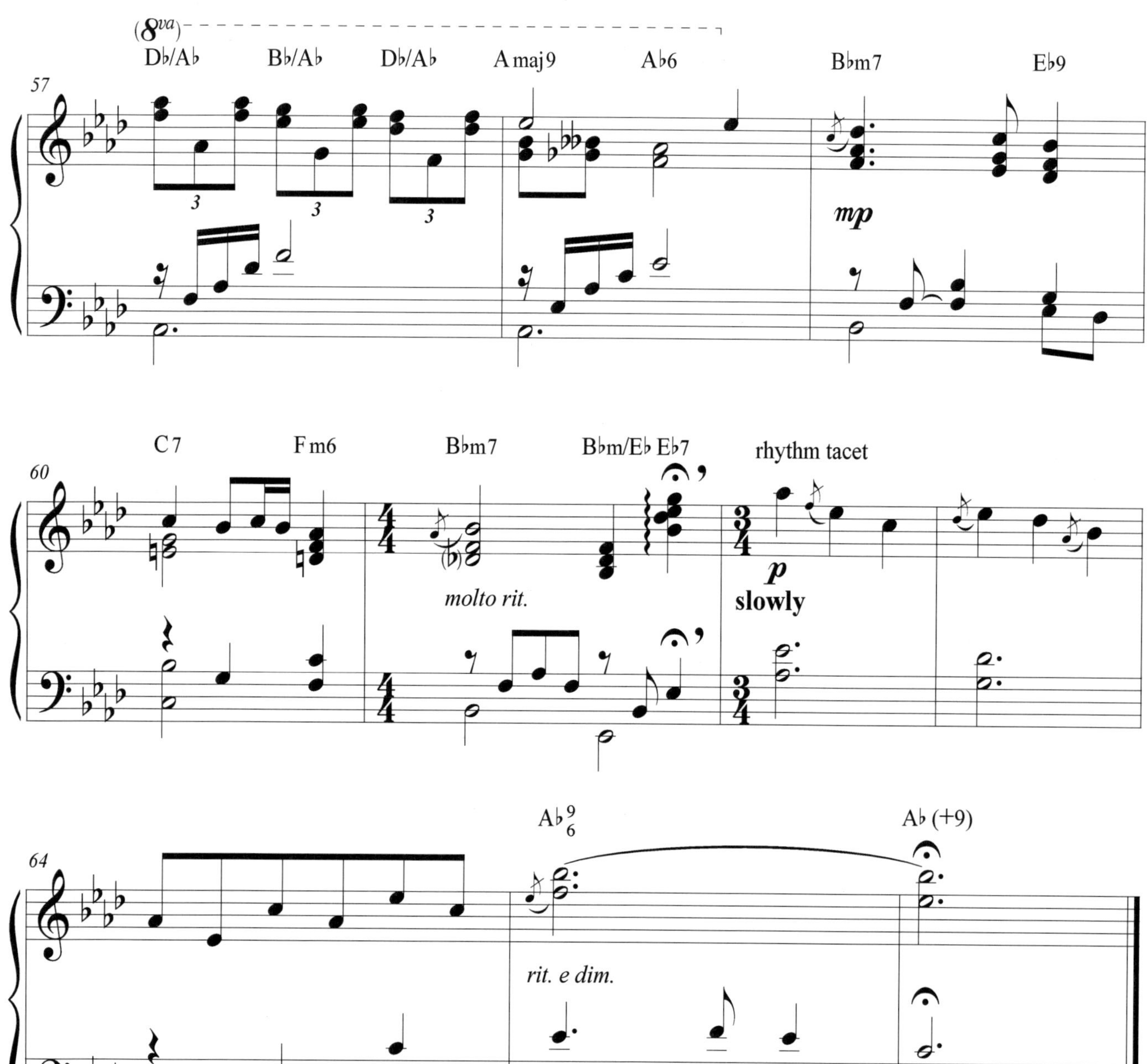
(8va)
D♭/A♭
B♭/A♭
D♭/A♭
A maj9
A♭6
B♭m7
E♭9
57
mp
C7
Fm6
B♭m7
B♭m/E♭ E♭7
rhythm tacet
60
molto rit.
p
slowly
64
A♭6/9
A♭ (+9)
rit. e dim.

Dear Little Stranger

CHARLES H. GABRIEL
Arr. Devan M. Archer

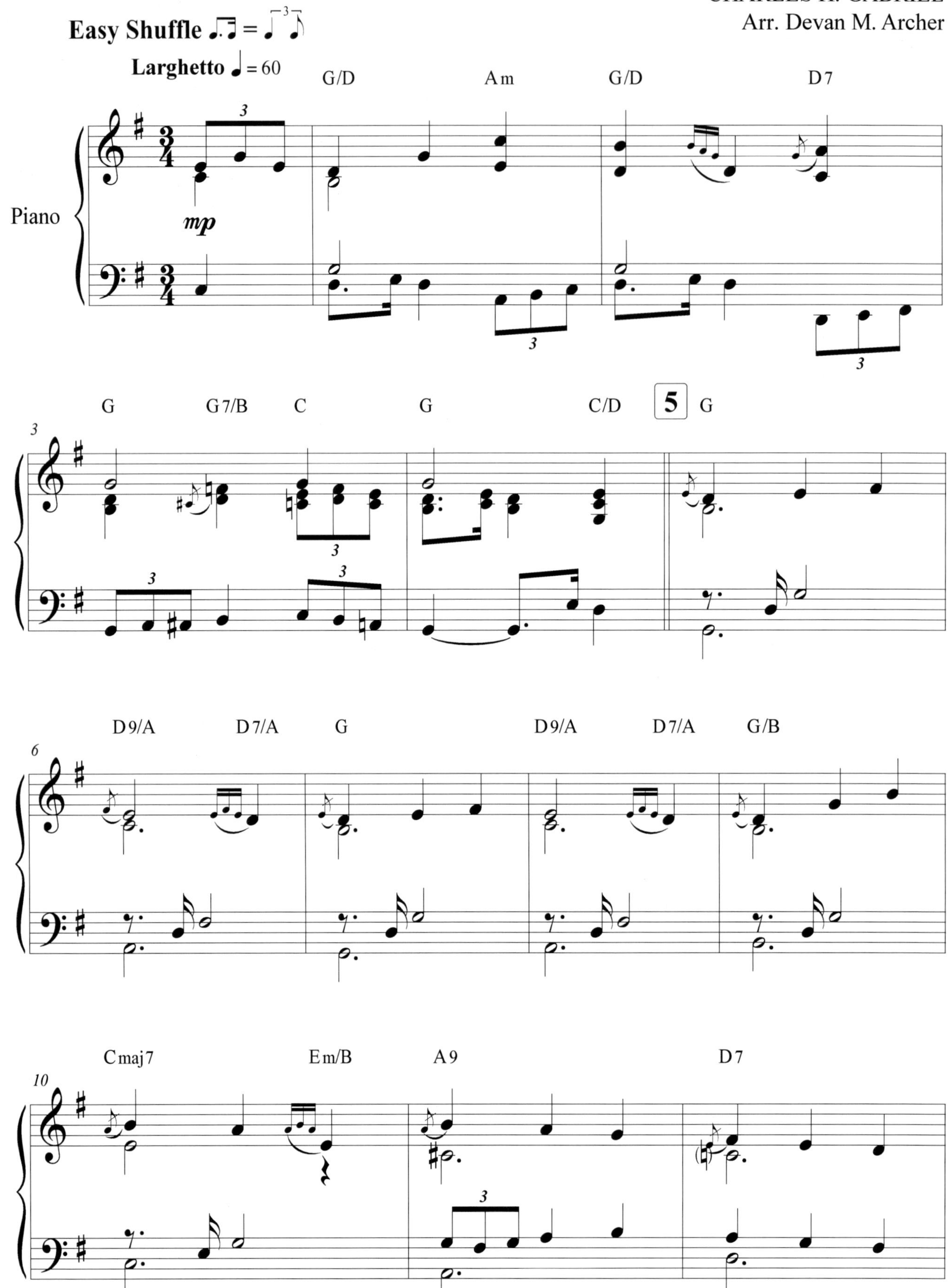

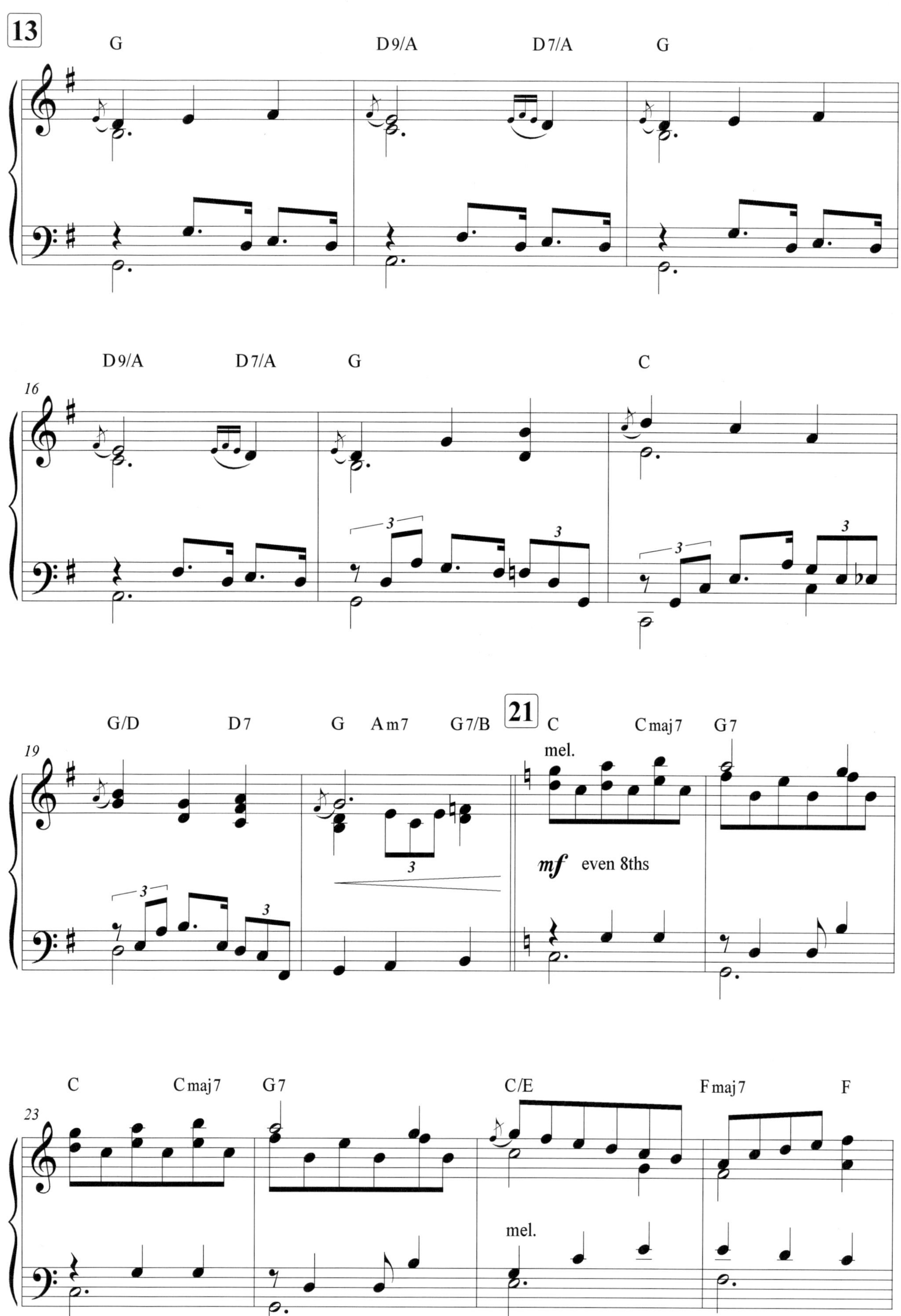
13
G
D 9/A
D 7/A
G
16
D 9/A
D 7/A
G
C
19
G/D
D 7
G
A m7
G 7/B
21
C
C maj 7
G 7
mel.
mf
even 8ths
23
C
C maj 7
G 7
C/E
F maj 7
F
mel.

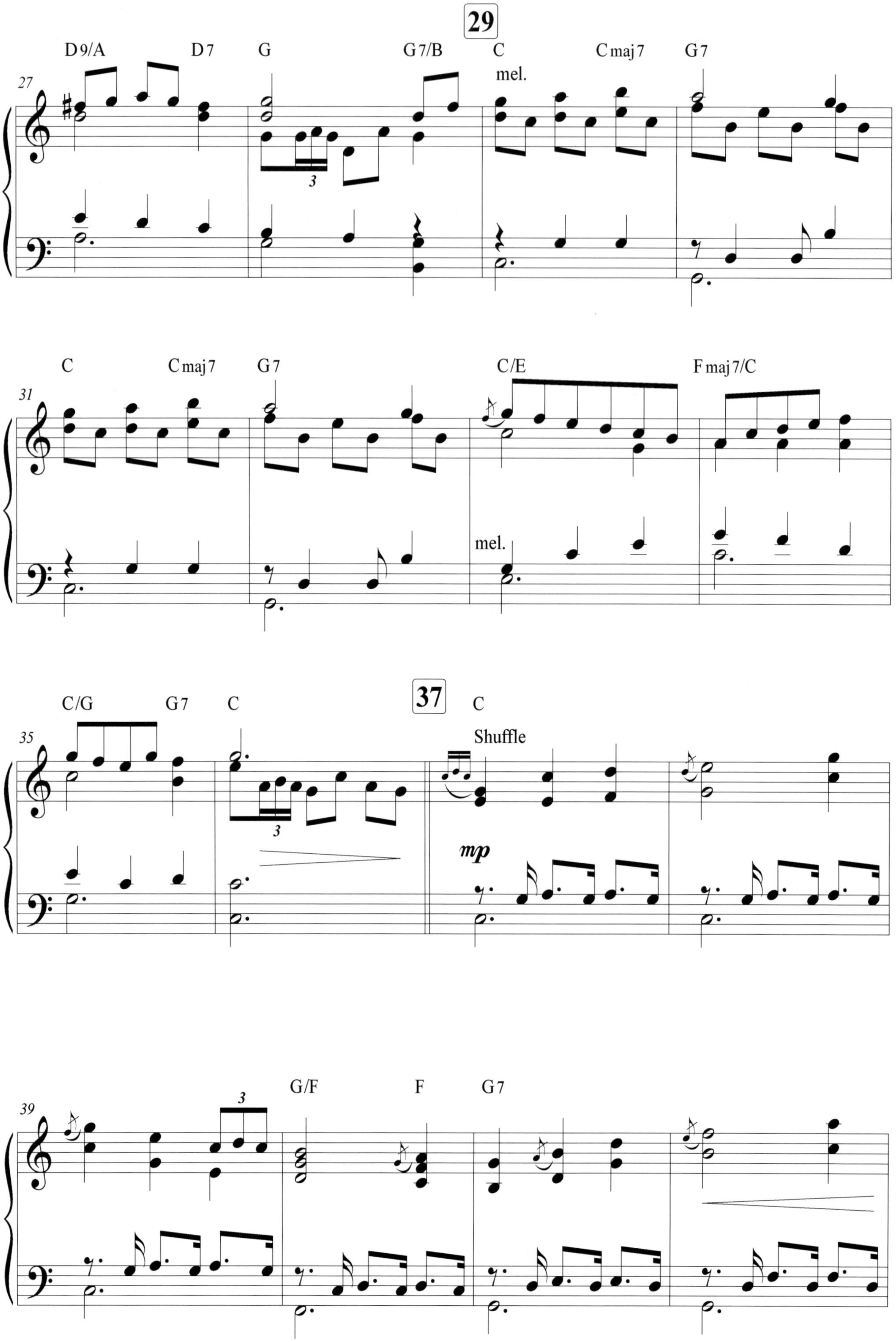

29

D9/A D7 G G7/B C Cmaj7 G7

27

mel.

3

C Cmaj7 G7 C/E Fmaj7/C

31

mel.

C/G G7 C **37** C

35

Shuffle

3

mp

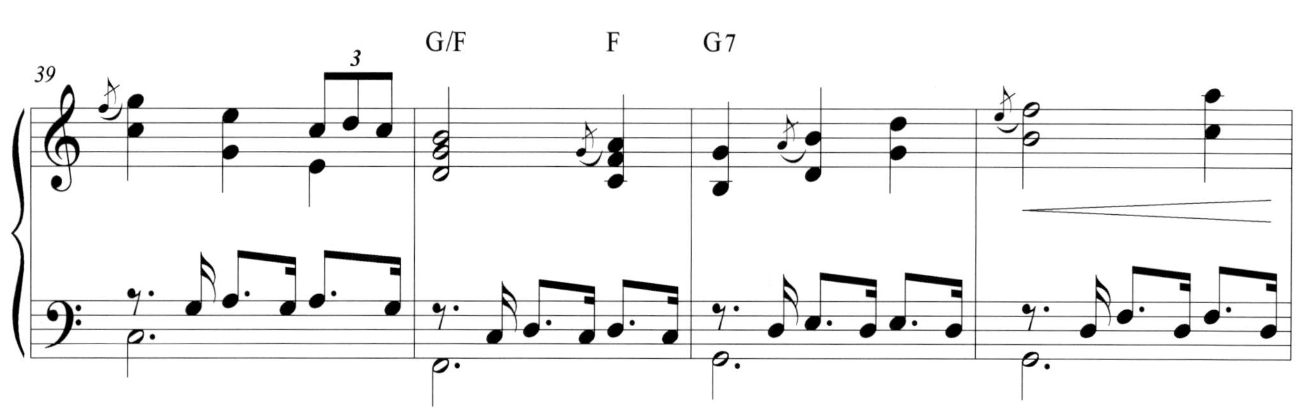

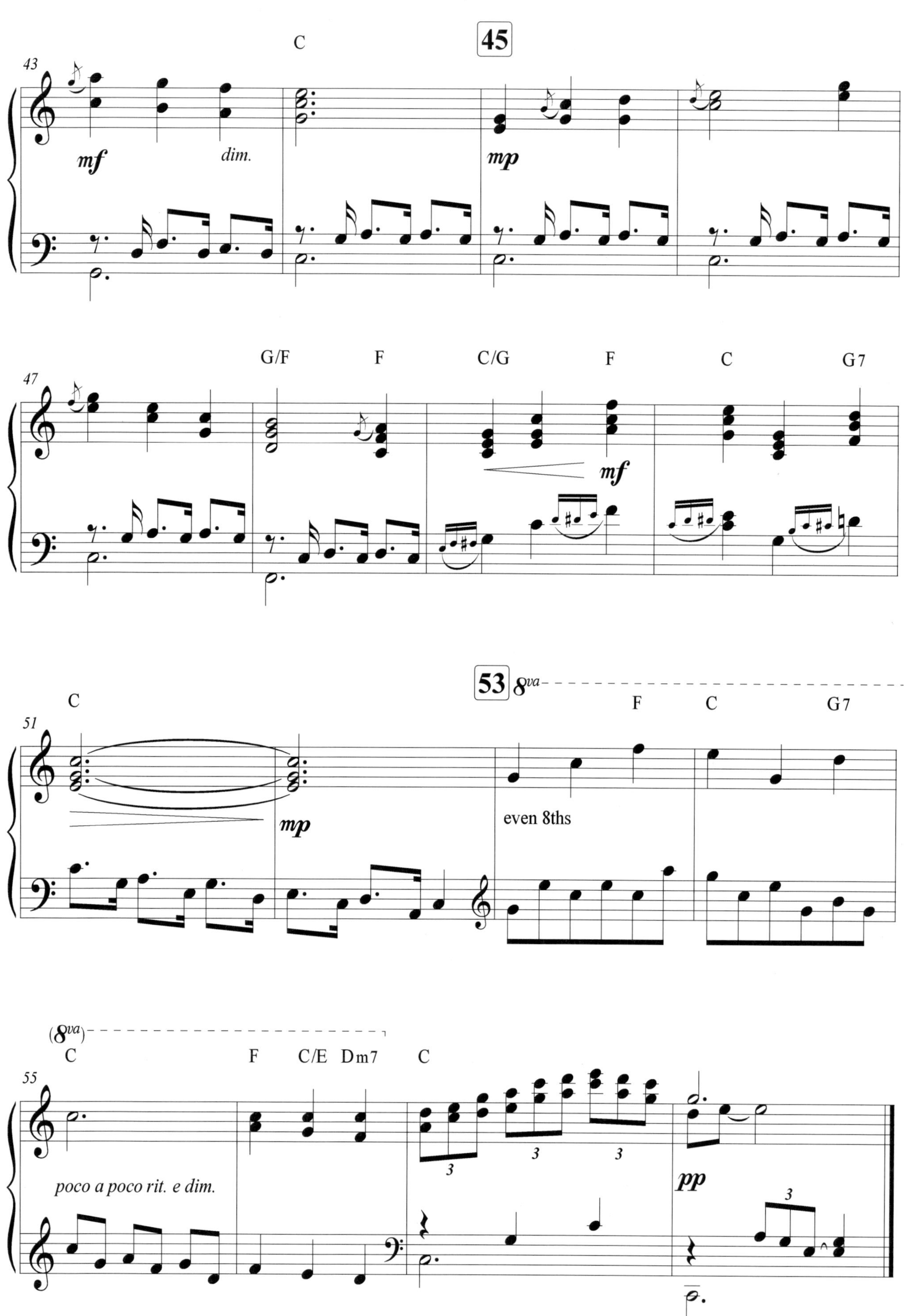
43
C
45
mf
dim.
mp
47
G/F
F
C/G
F
C
G7
mf
51
C
53
8va
F
C
G7
mp
even 8ths
(8va)
55
C
F
C/E
Dm7
C
poco a poco rit. e dim.
3
pp

God Rest Ye Merry, Gentlemen

18TH CEN. ENGLISH CAROL
Arr. Devan M. Archer

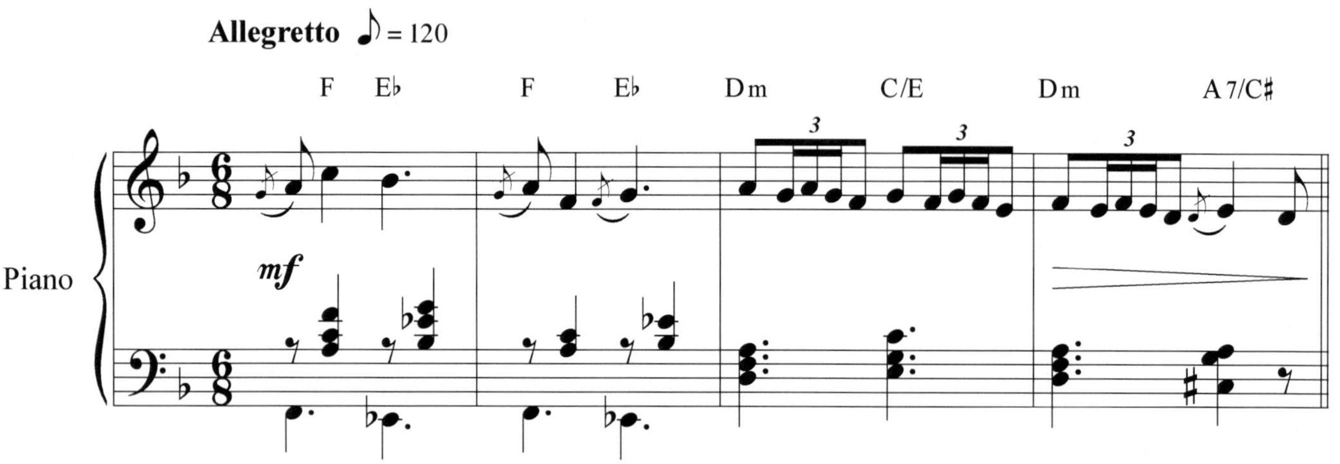

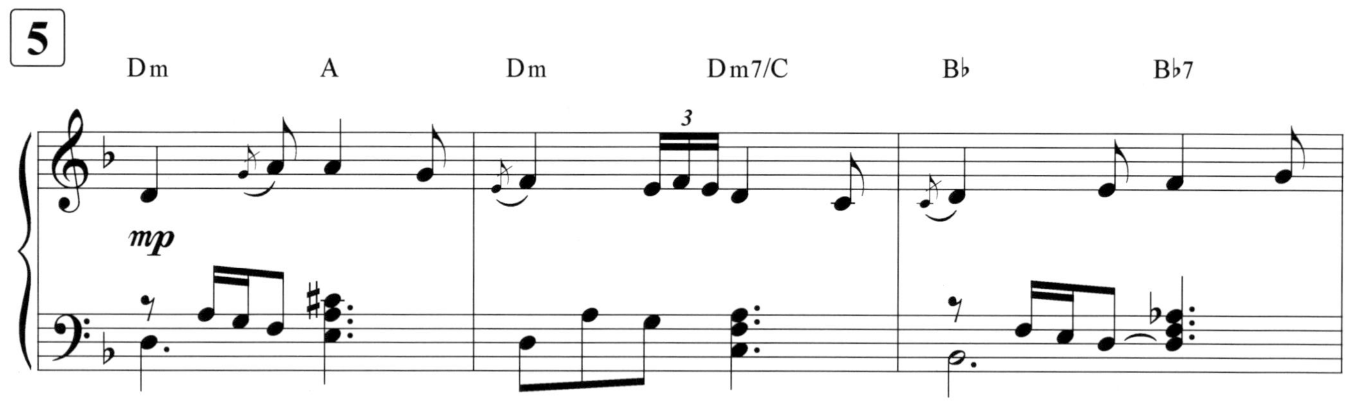

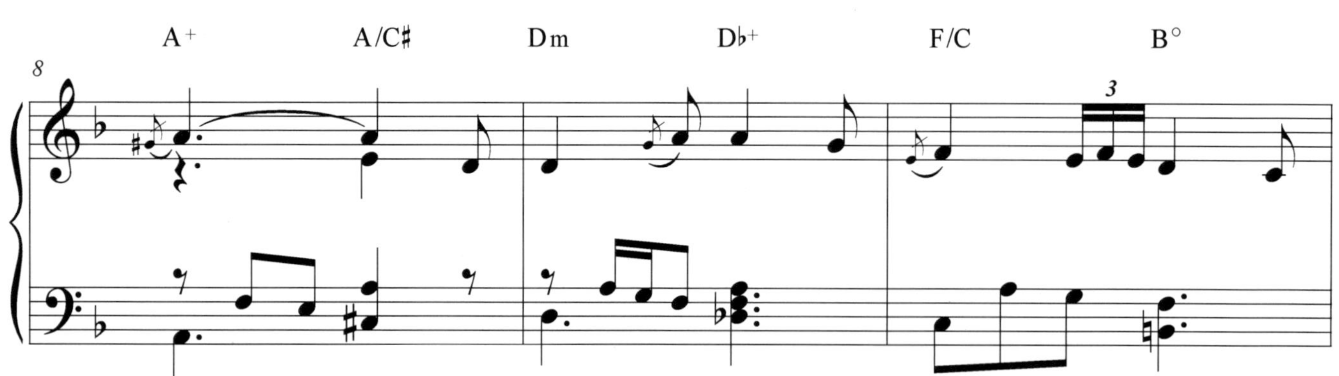

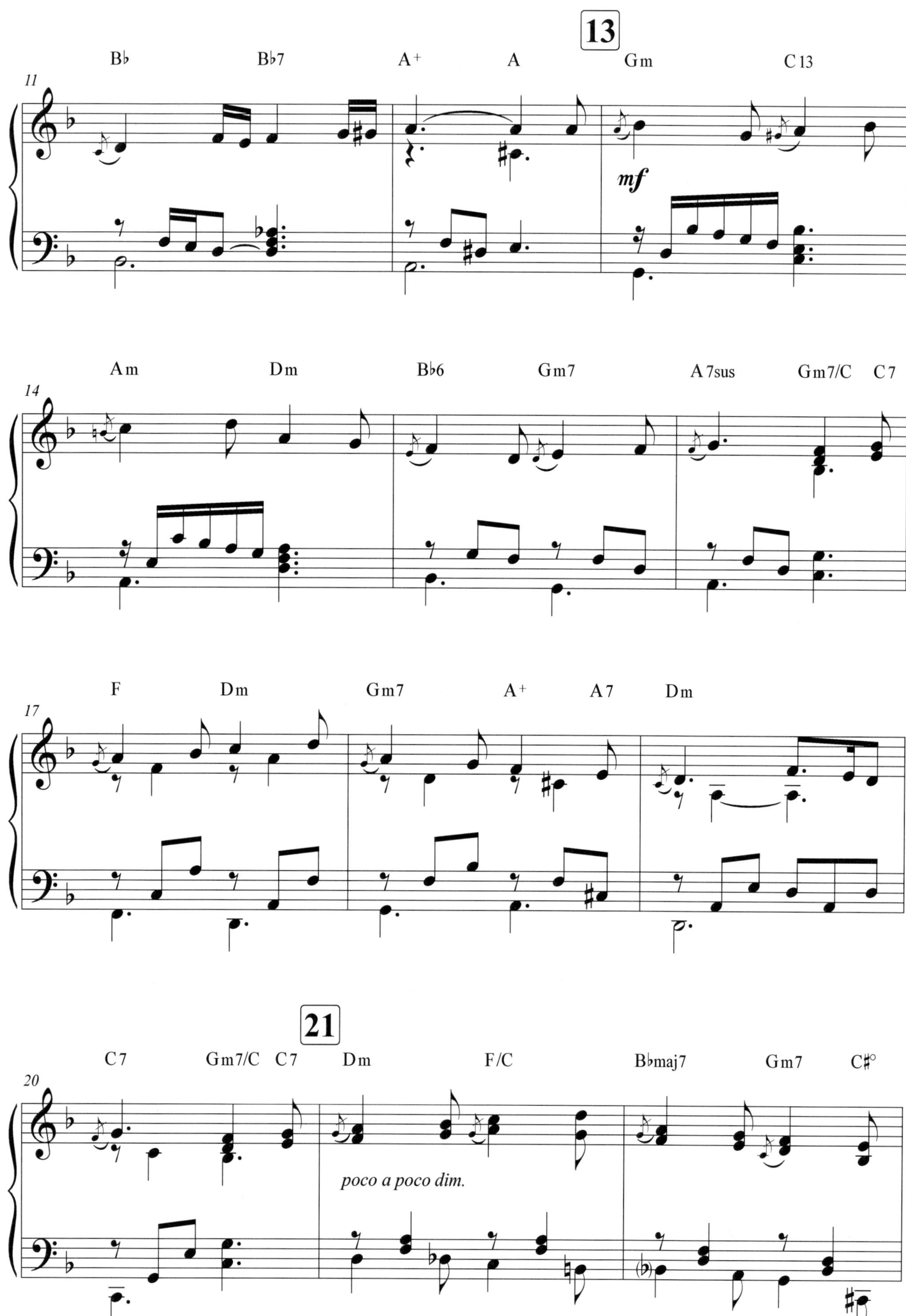
13
B♭ B♭7 A+ A Gm C13
mf
Am Dm B♭6 Gm7 A7sus Gm7/C C7
F Dm Gm7 A+ A7 Dm
21
C7 Gm7/C C7 Dm F/C B♭maj7 Gm7 C♯°
poco a poco dim.

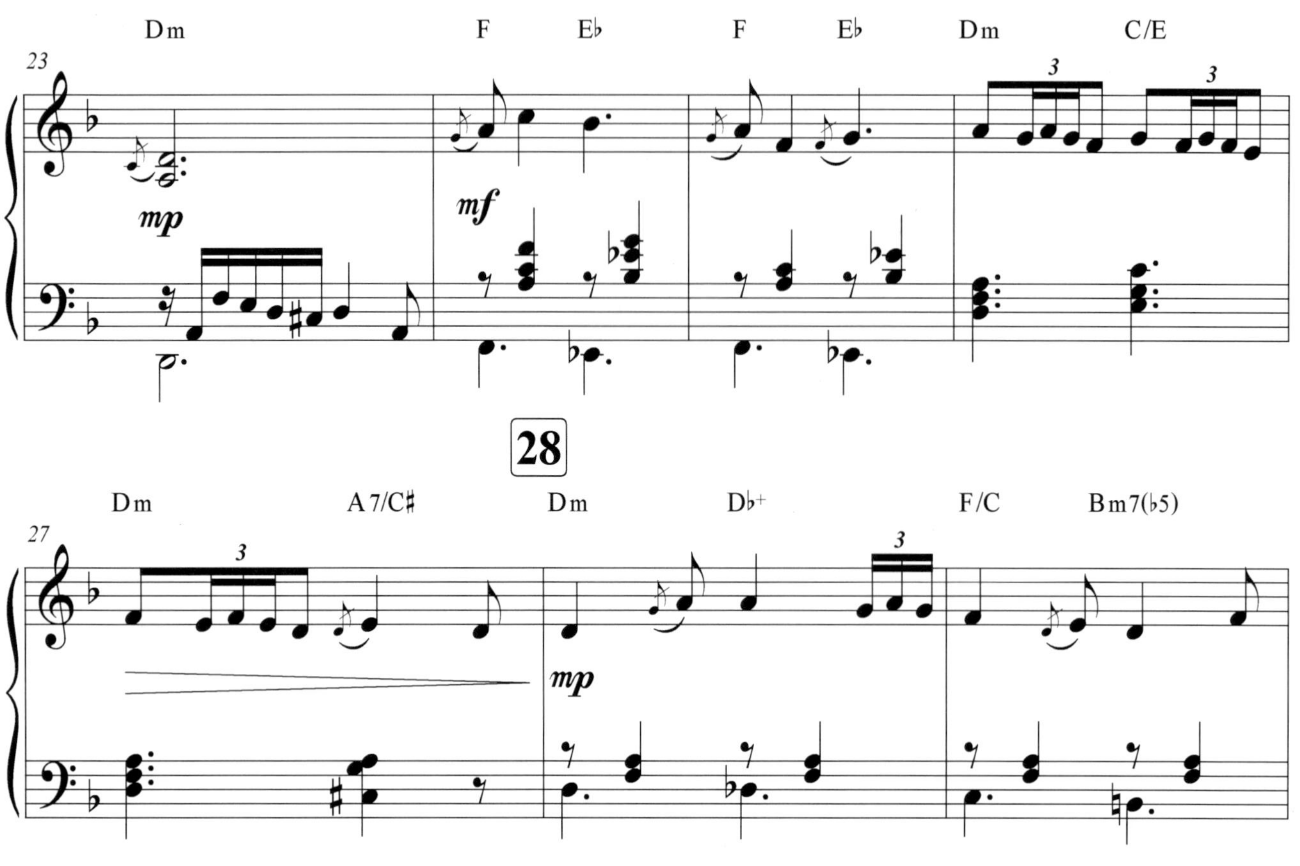
Dm F E♭ F E♭ Dm C/E
23
mp
mf
28
Dm A7/C♯ Dm D♭+ F/C Bm7(♭5)
27
mp
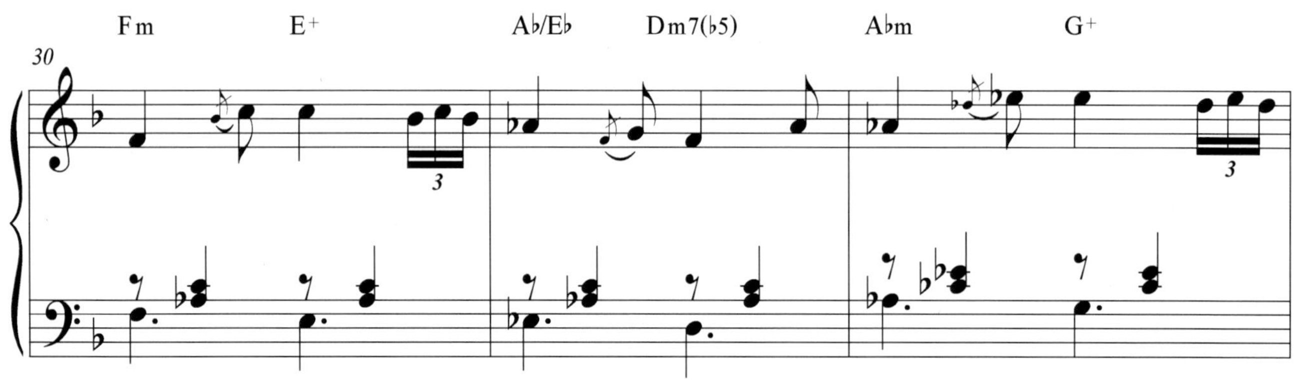
Fm E+ A♭/E♭ Dm7(♭5) A♭m G+
30
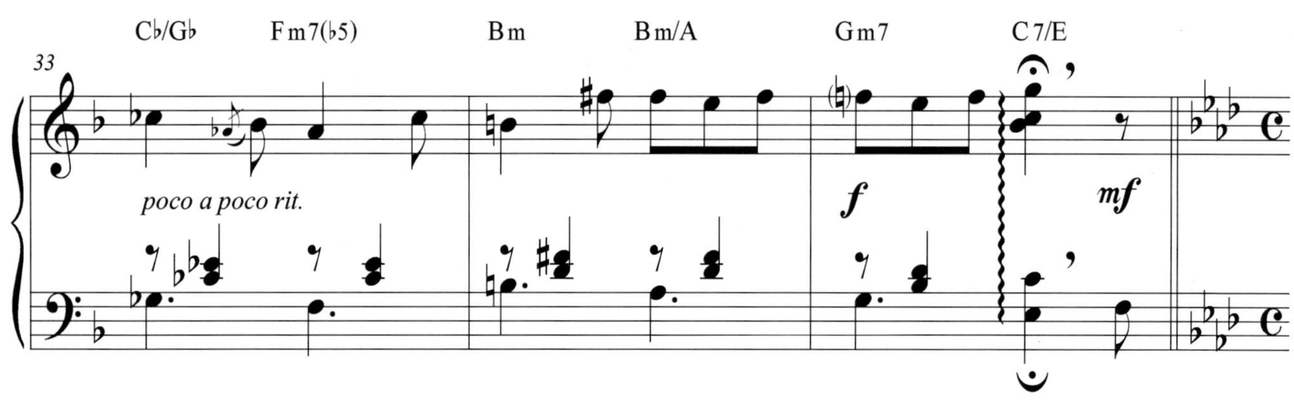
C♭/G♭ Fm7(♭5) Bm Bm/A Gm7 C7/E
33
poco a poco rit.
f
mf

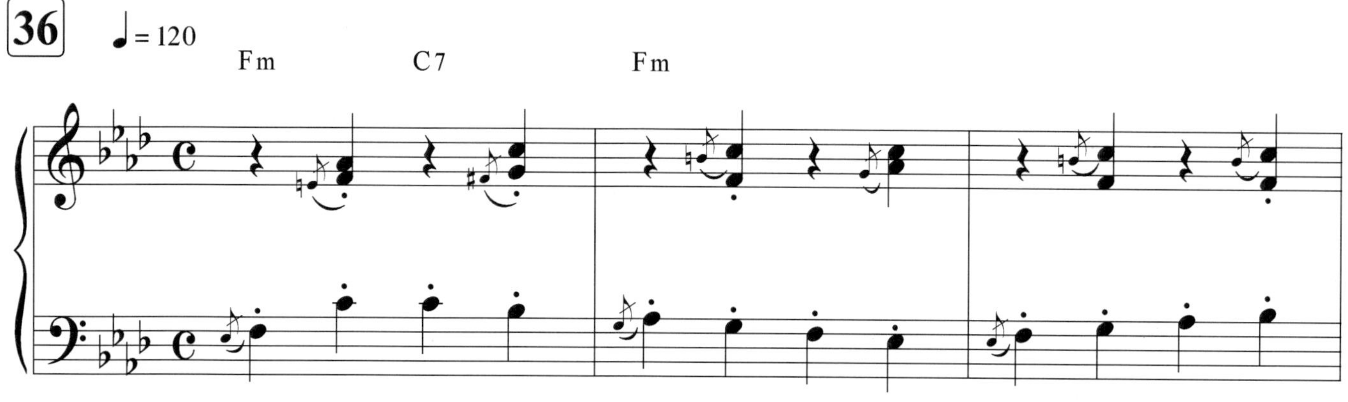
36
♩= 120
Fm
C7
Fm

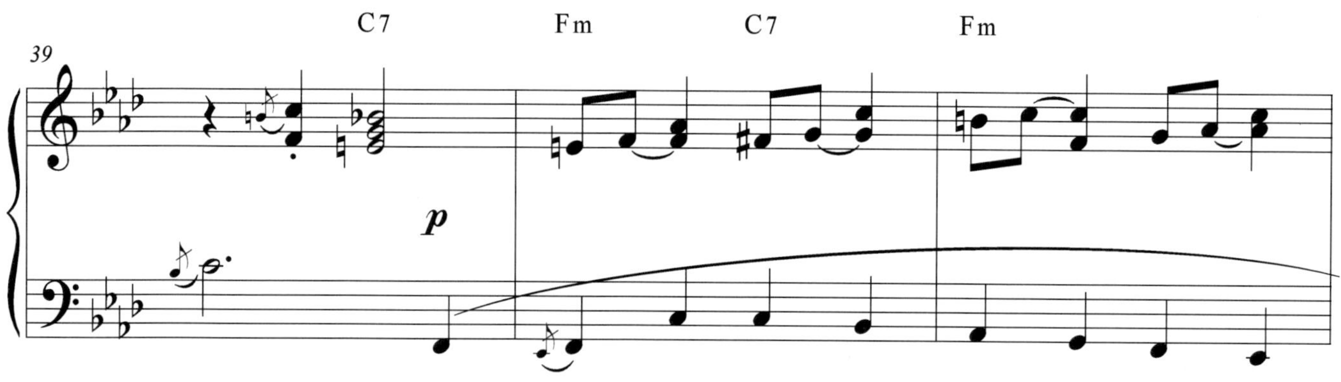
39
C7
Fm
C7
Fm
p

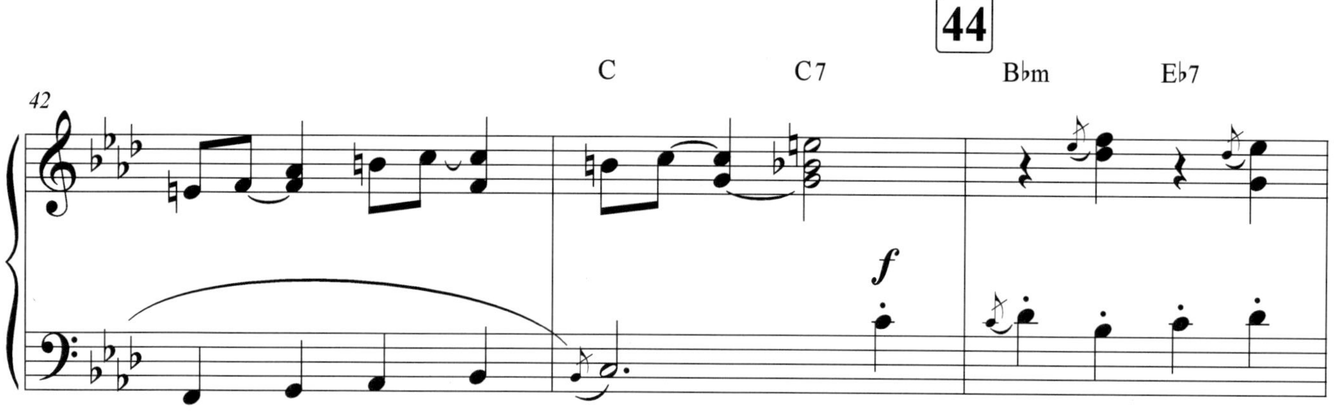
44
42
C
C7
B♭m
E♭7
f

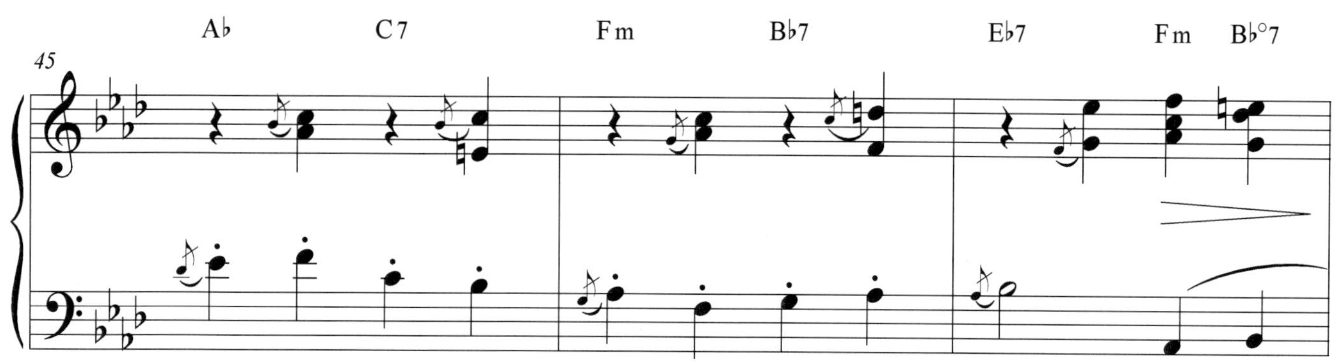
45
A♭
C7
Fm
B♭7
E♭7
Fm
B♭°7

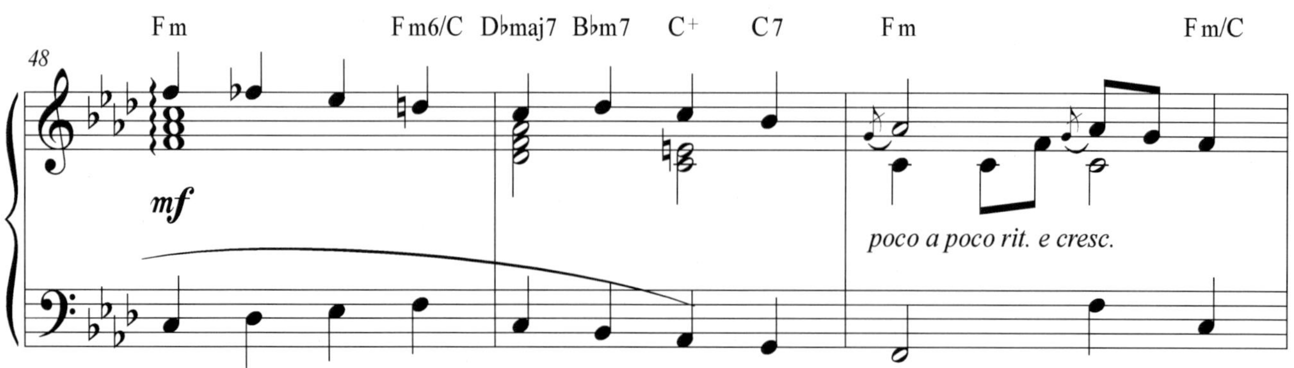
Fm
Fm6/C
D♭maj7
B♭m7
C+
C7
Fm
Fm/C
48
mf
poco a poco rit. e cresc.
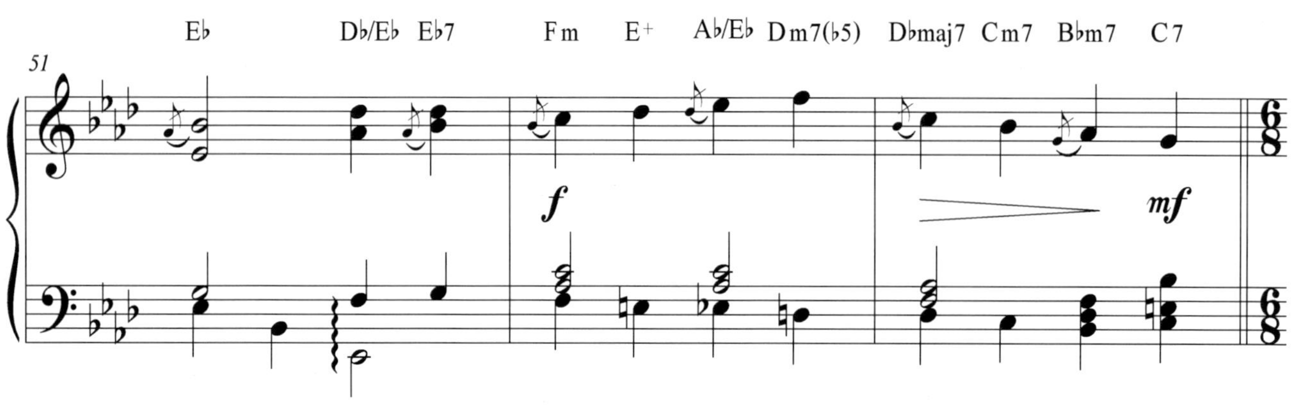
E♭
D♭/E♭
E♭7
Fm
E+
A♭/E♭
Dm7(♭5)
D♭maj7
Cm7
B♭m7
C7
51
f
mf
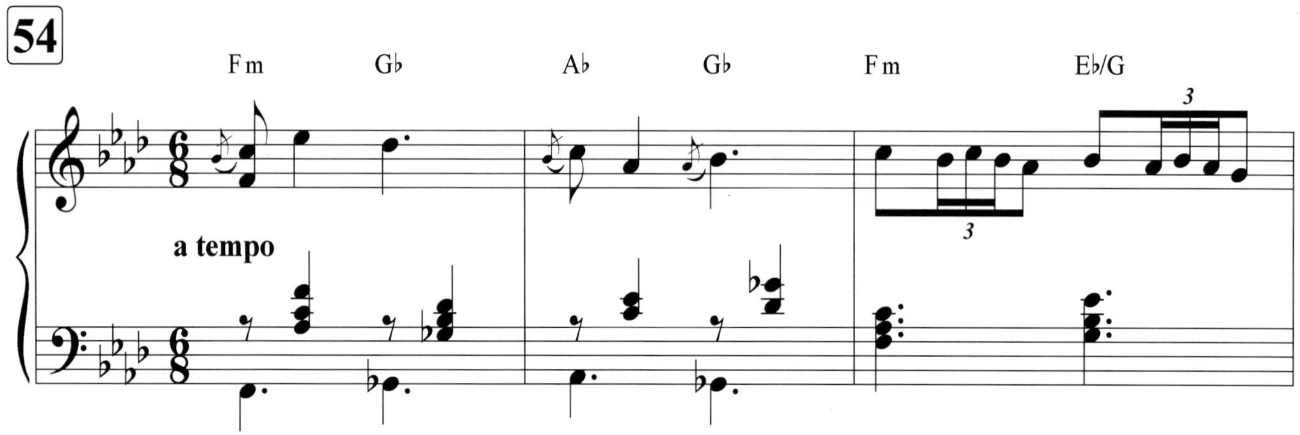
54
Fm
G♭
A♭
G♭
Fm
E♭/G
a tempo
3
3
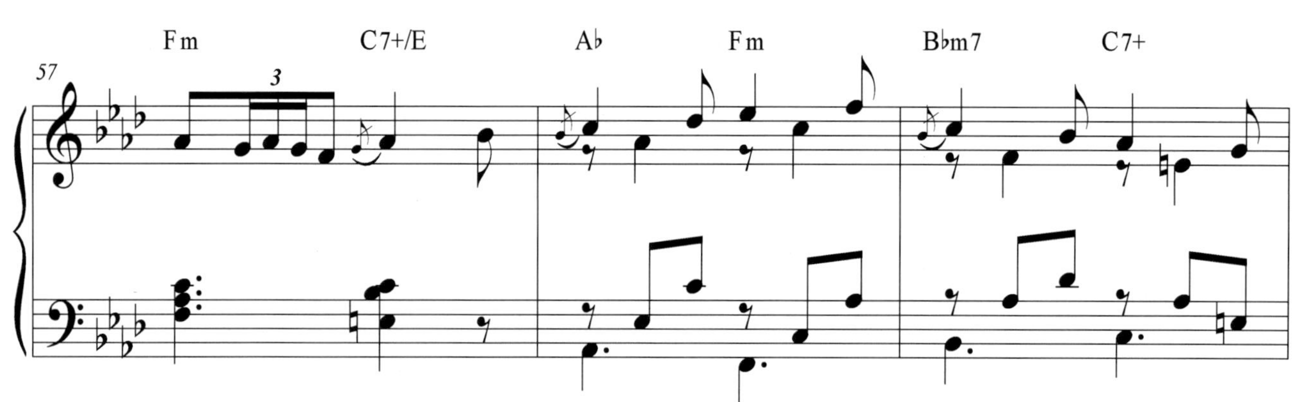
Fm
C7+/E
A♭
Fm
B♭m7
C7+
57
3

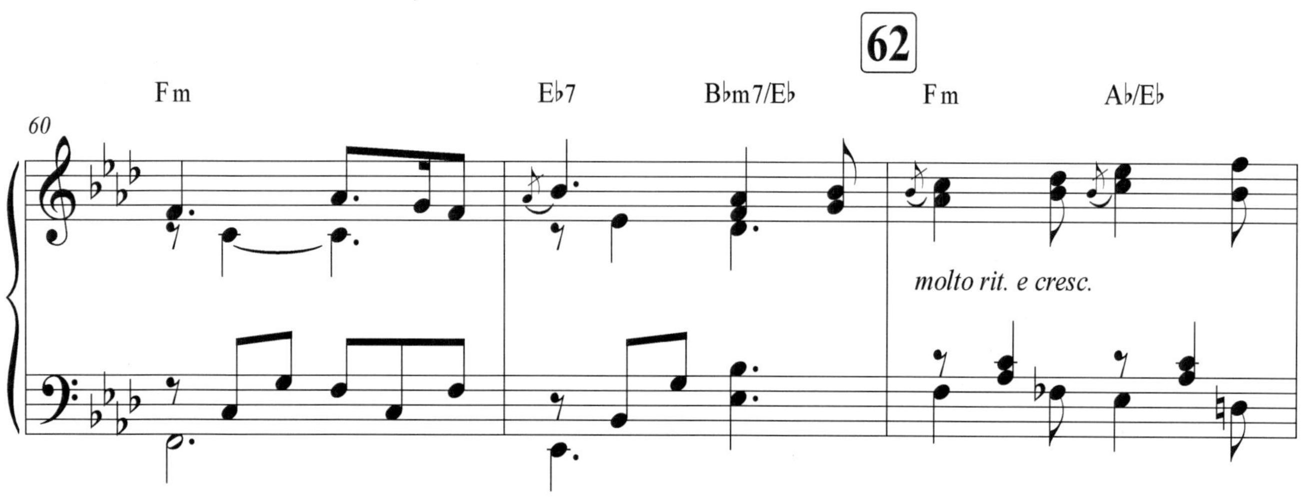
62
Fm
E♭7
B♭m7/E♭
Fm
A♭/E♭
60
molto rit. e cresc.

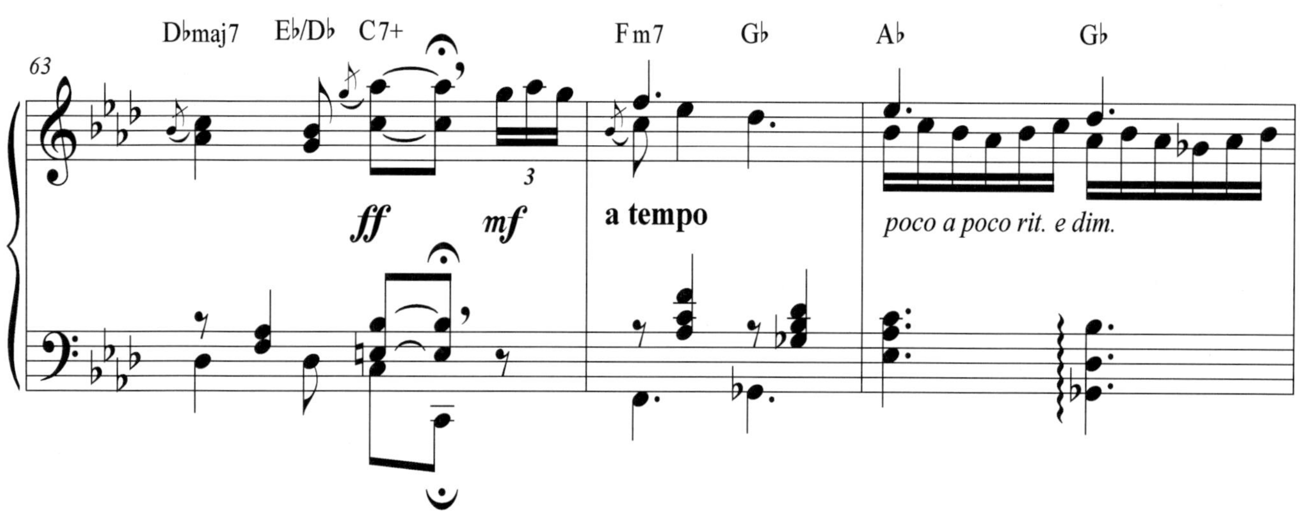
D♭maj7
E♭/D♭
C7+
Fm7
G♭
A♭
G♭
63
3
ff
mf
a tempo
poco a poco rit. e dim.

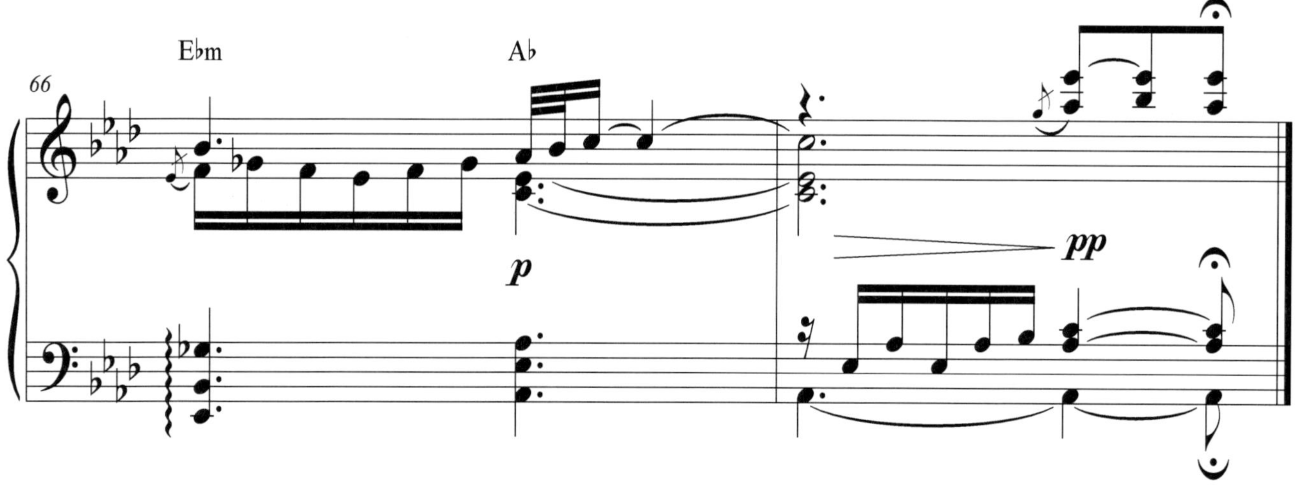
E♭m
A♭
66
p
pp

Good King Wenceslas

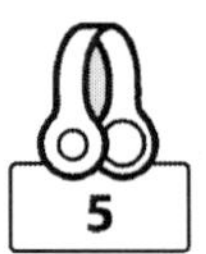

TRADITIONAL
Arr. Devan M. Archer

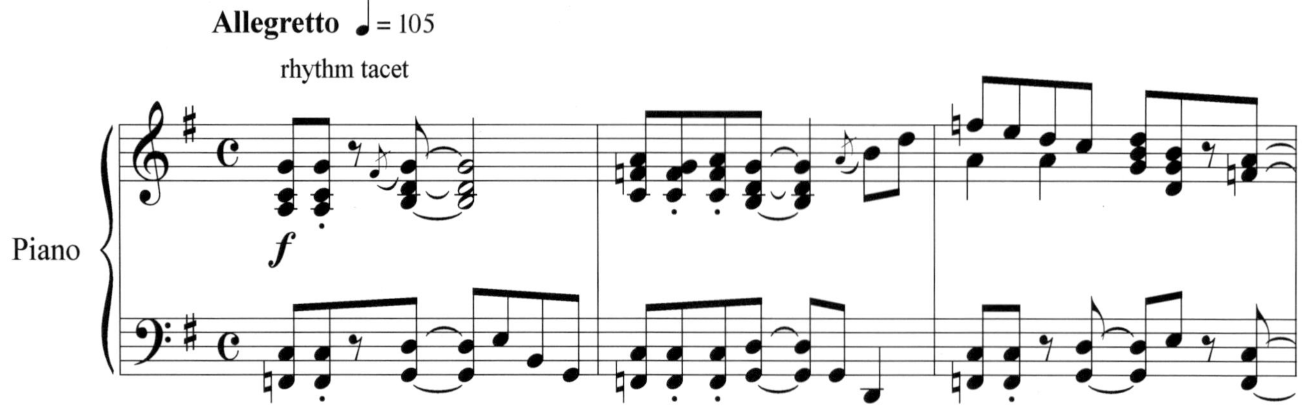

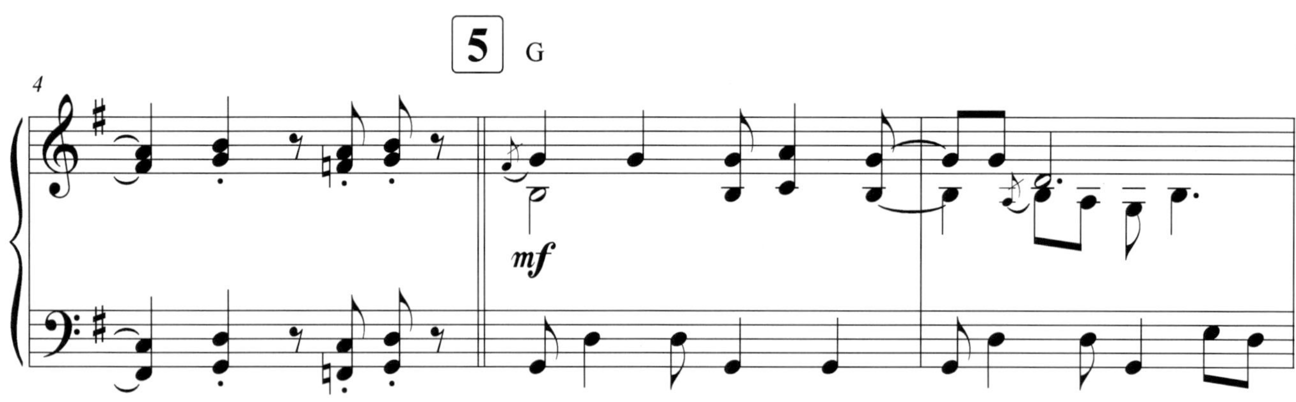

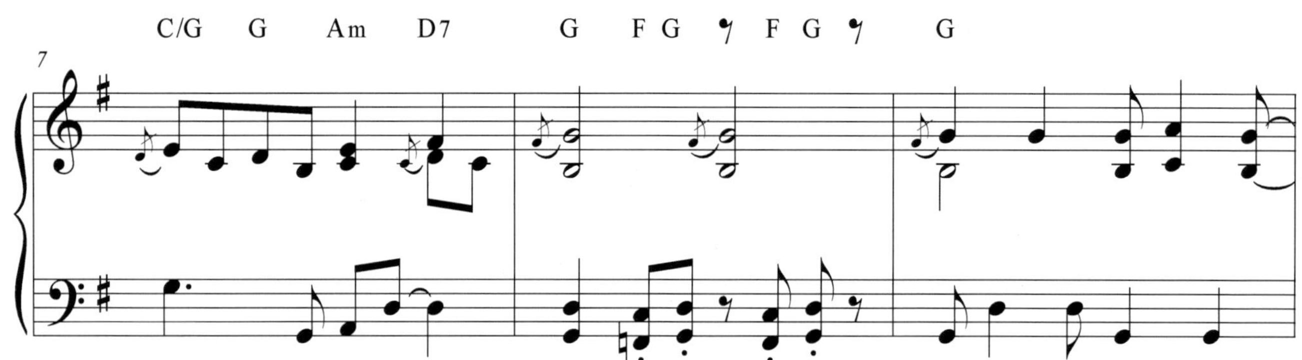

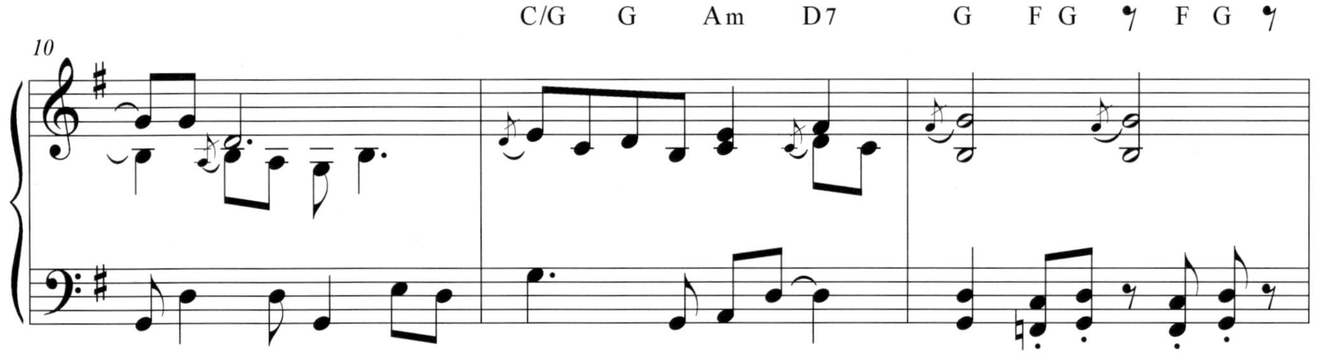
C/G G Am D7 G F G F G
10

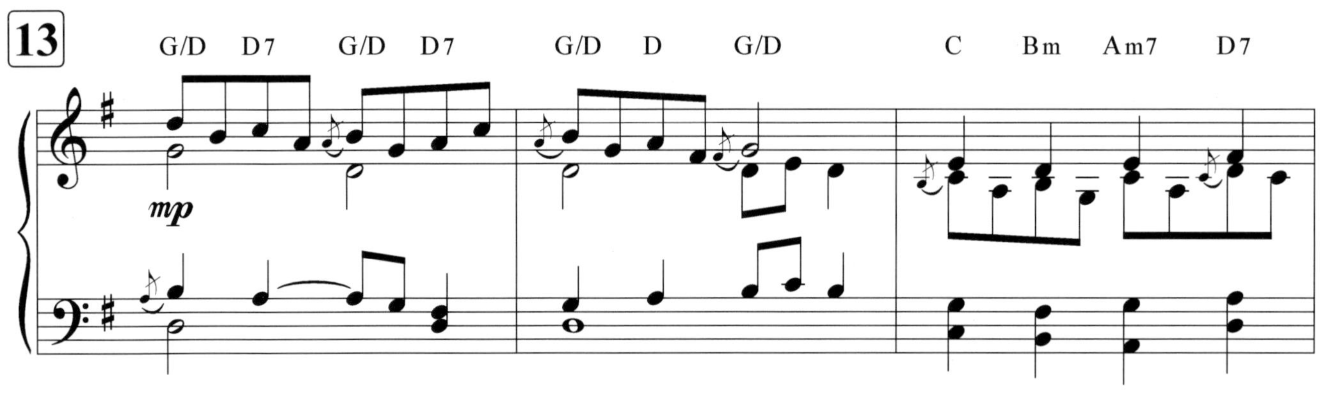
13
G/D D7 G/D D7 G/D D G/D C Bm Am7 D7
mp

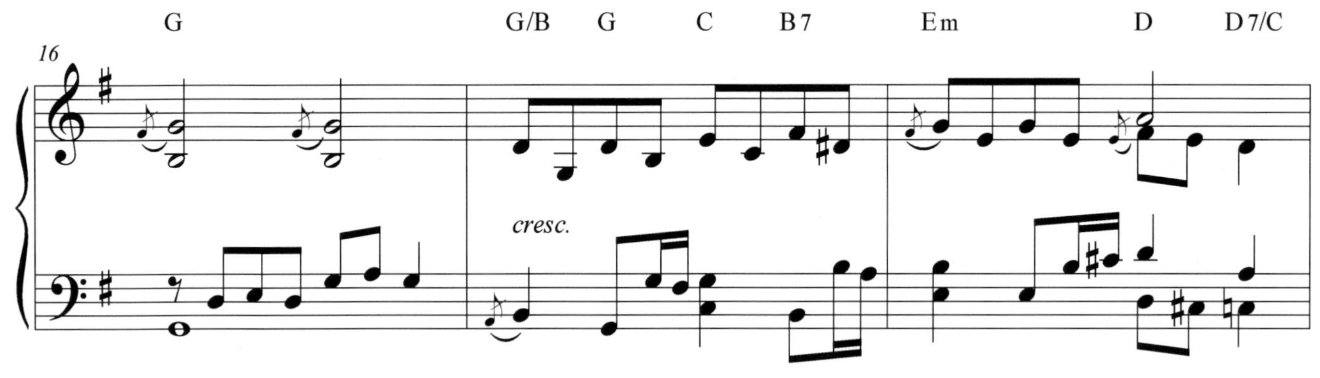
G G/B G C B7 Em D D7/C
16
cresc.

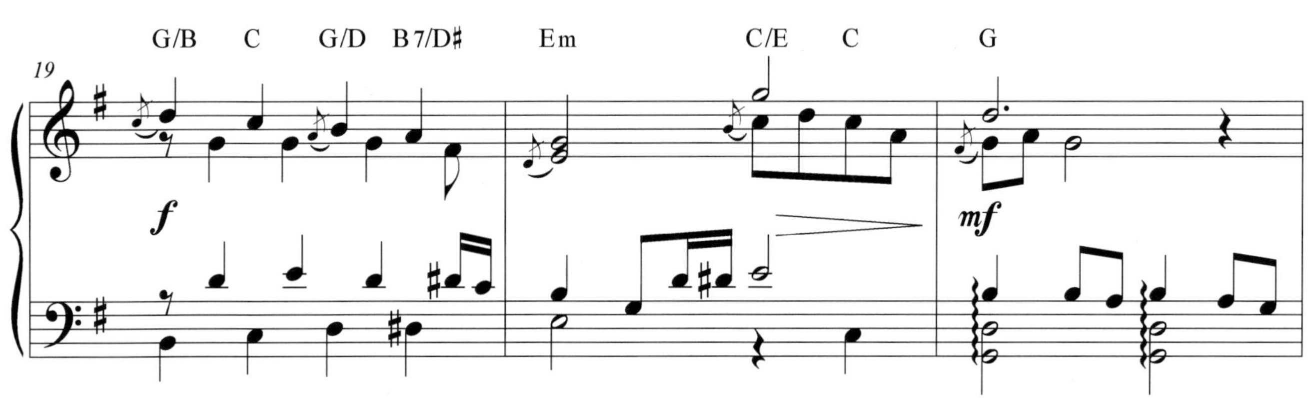
G/B C G/D B7/D♯ Em C/E C G
19
f
mf

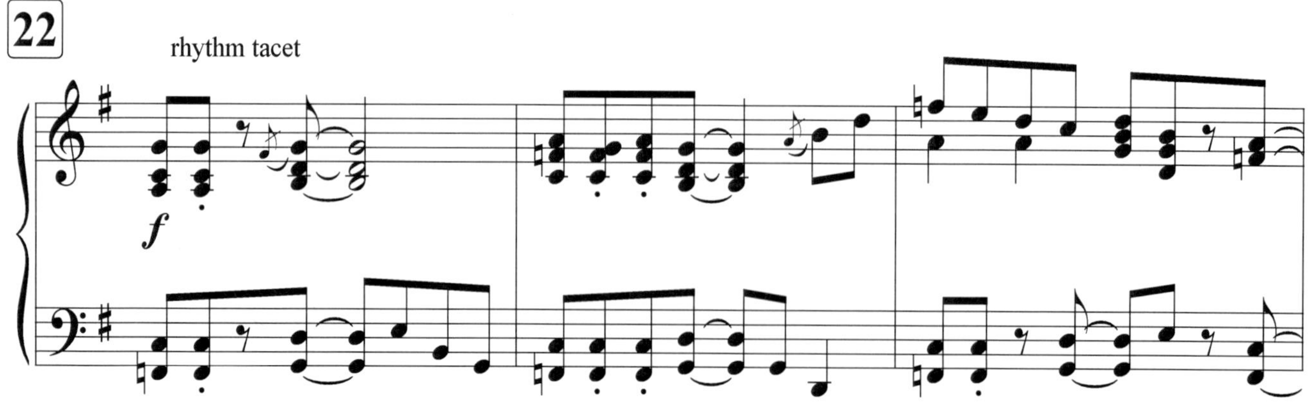
22
rhythm tacet
f

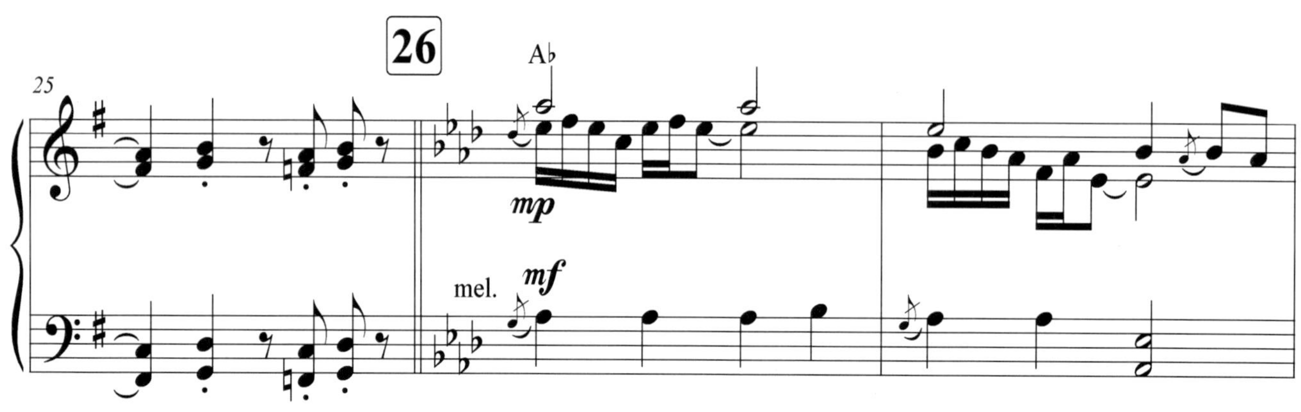
26
A♭
25
mp
mel.
mf

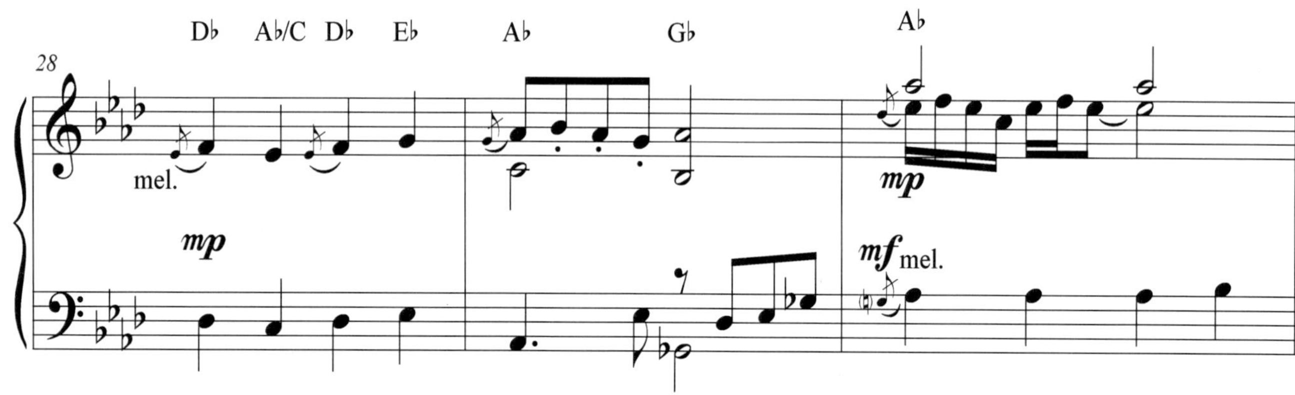
D♭
A♭/C
D♭
E♭
A♭
G♭
A♭
28
mel.
mp
mf
mel.
mp

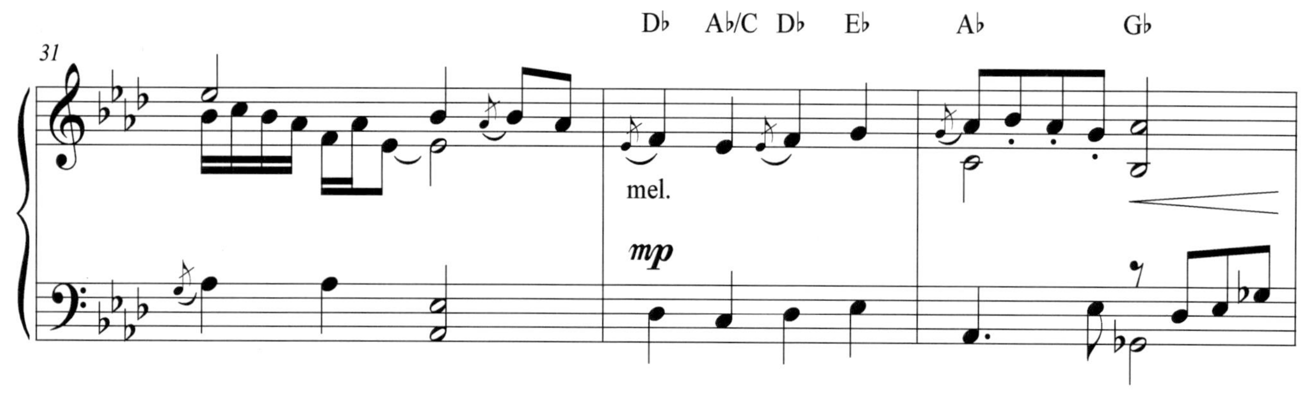
D♭
A♭/C
D♭
E♭
A♭
G♭
31
mel.
mp

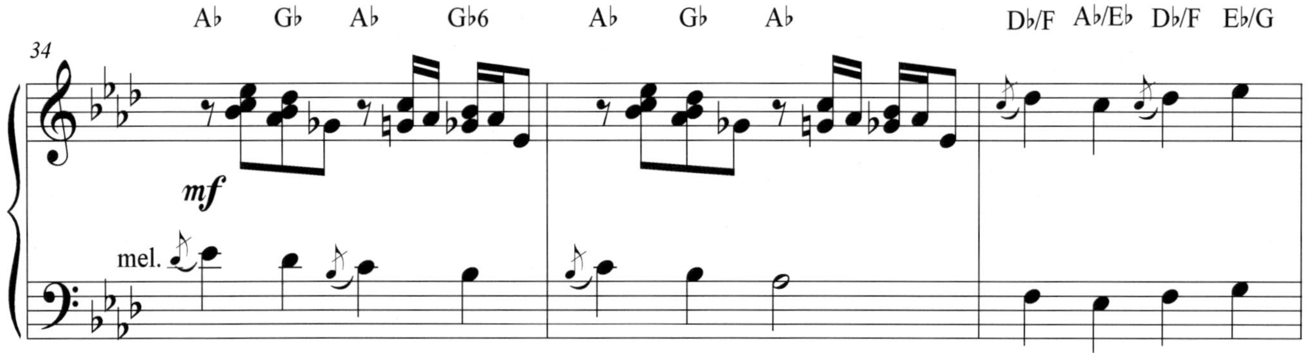
34
A♭ G♭ A♭ G♭6 A♭ G♭ A♭ D♭/F A♭/E♭ D♭/F E♭/G
mf
mel.

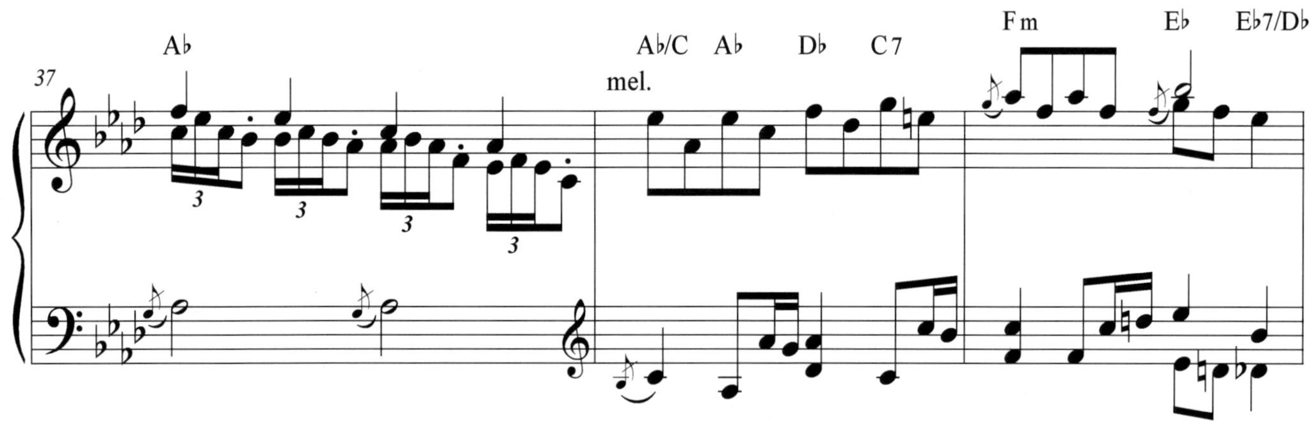
37
A♭ A♭/C A♭ D♭ C7 Fm E♭ E♭7/D♭
mel.

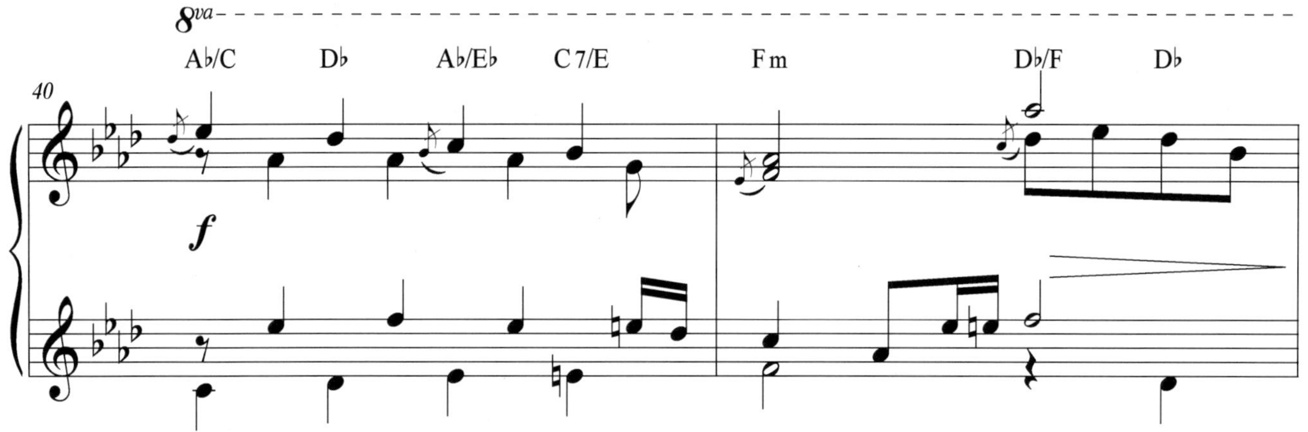
40
8va
A♭/C D♭ A♭/E♭ C7/E Fm D♭/F D♭
f

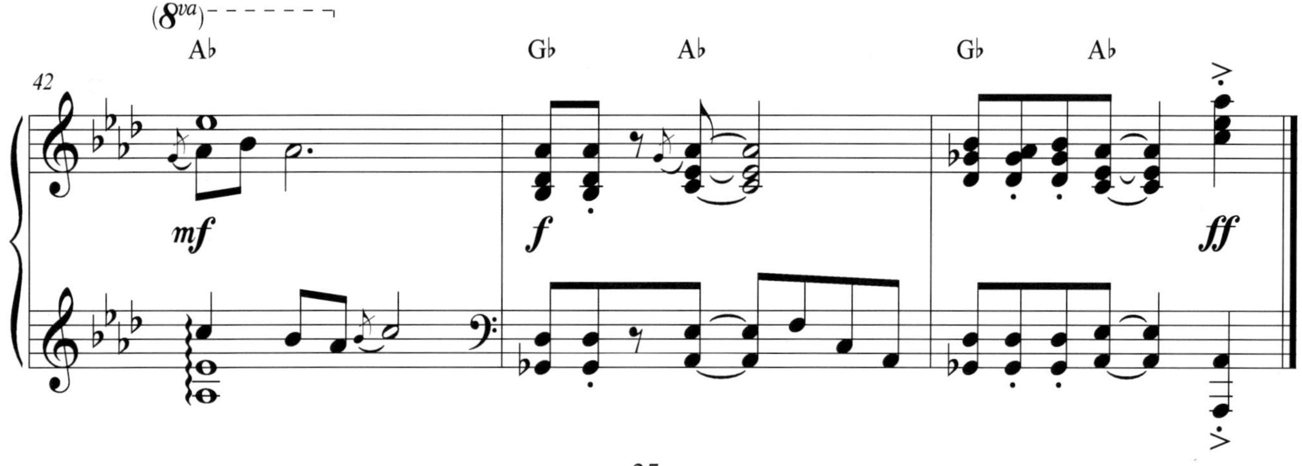
42
(8va)
A♭ G♭ A♭ G♭ A♭
mf
f
ff

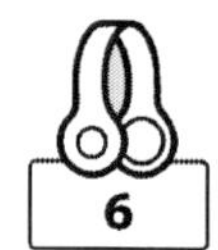

Jesus Came Long Ago

FROM BRAHMS' "CRADLE SONG"
Arr. Devan M. Archer

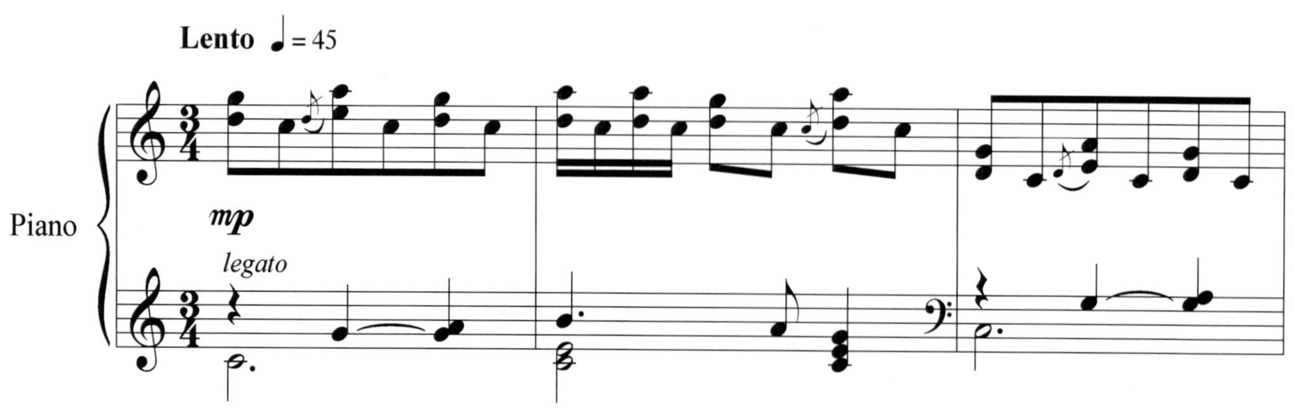

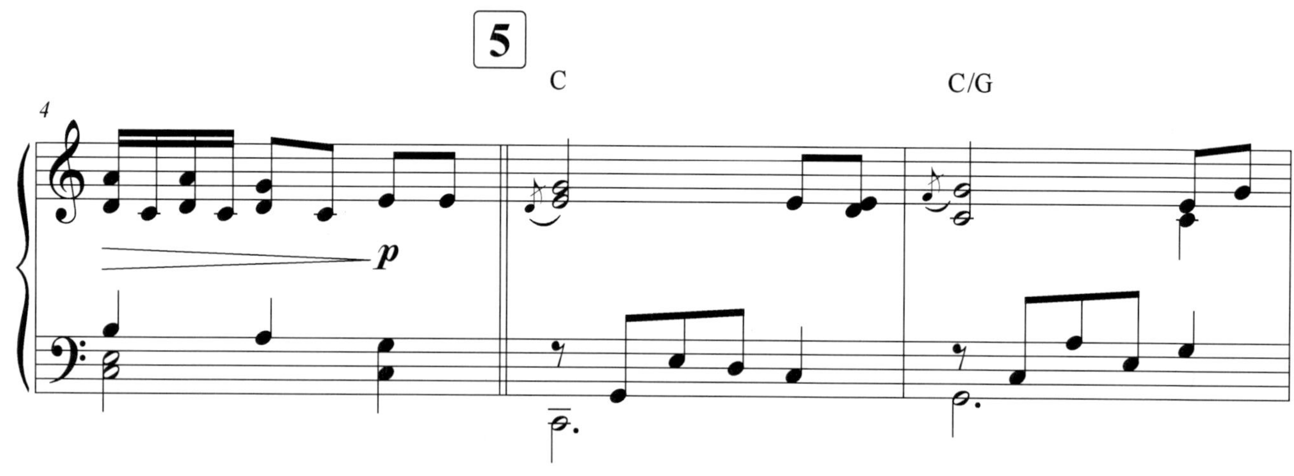

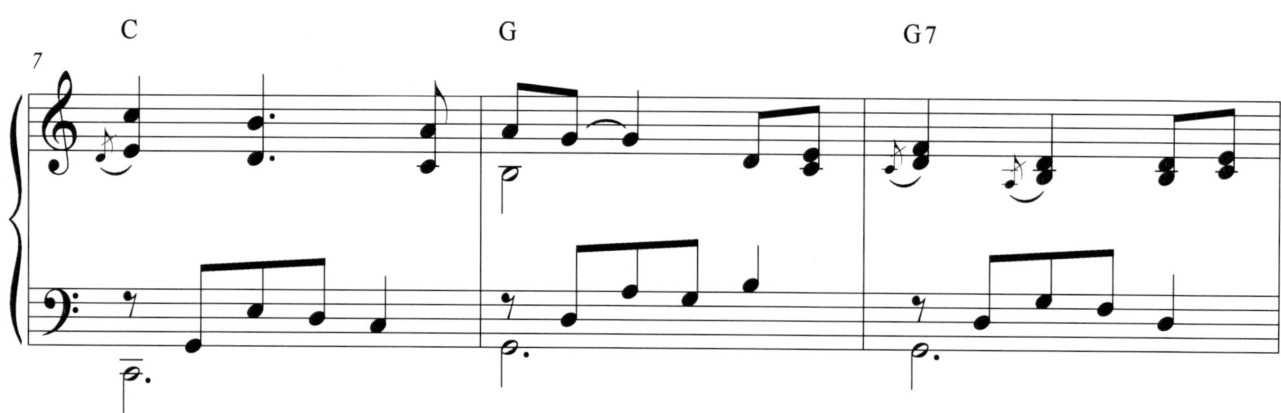

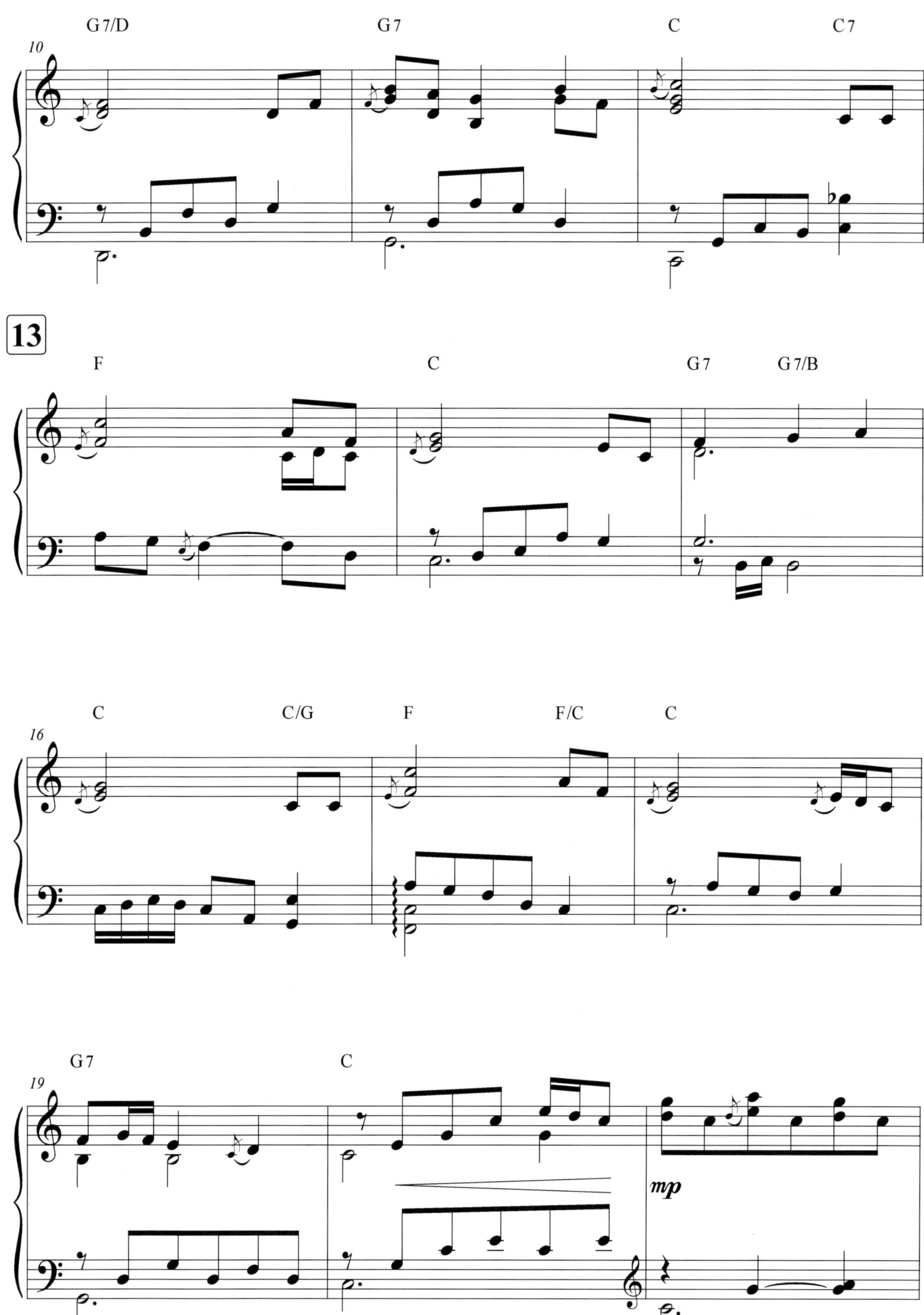
G7/D
G7
C
C7
10
13
F
C
G7
G7/B
C
C/G
F
F/C
C
16
G7
C
19
mp

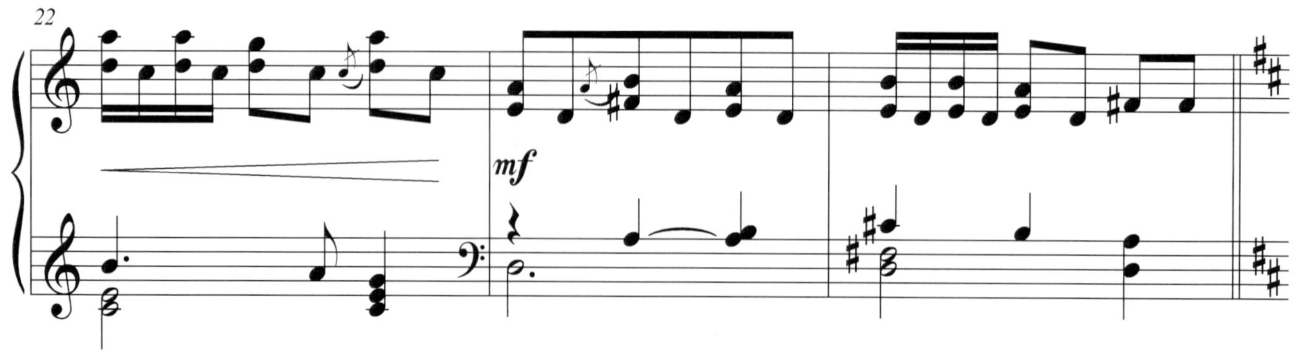
22
mf

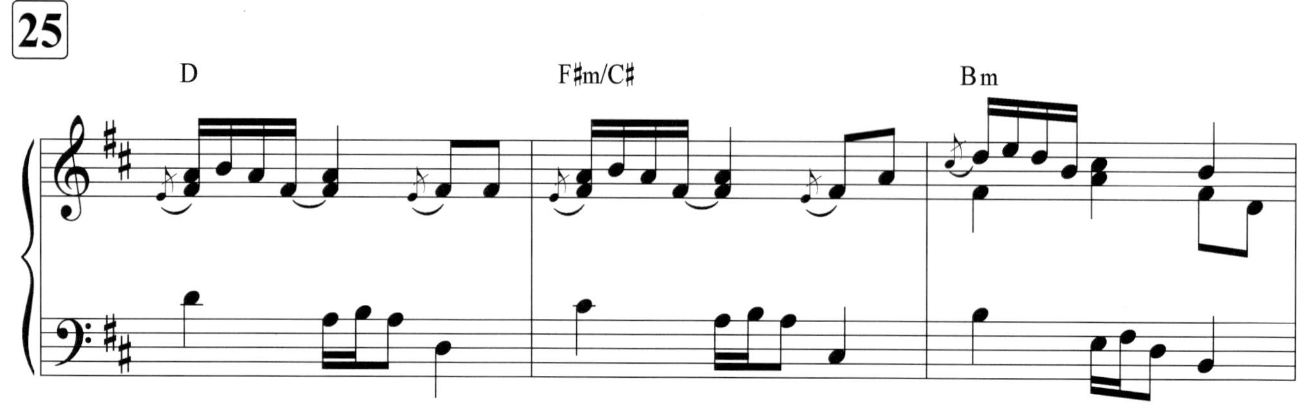
25
D
F♯m/C♯
Bm

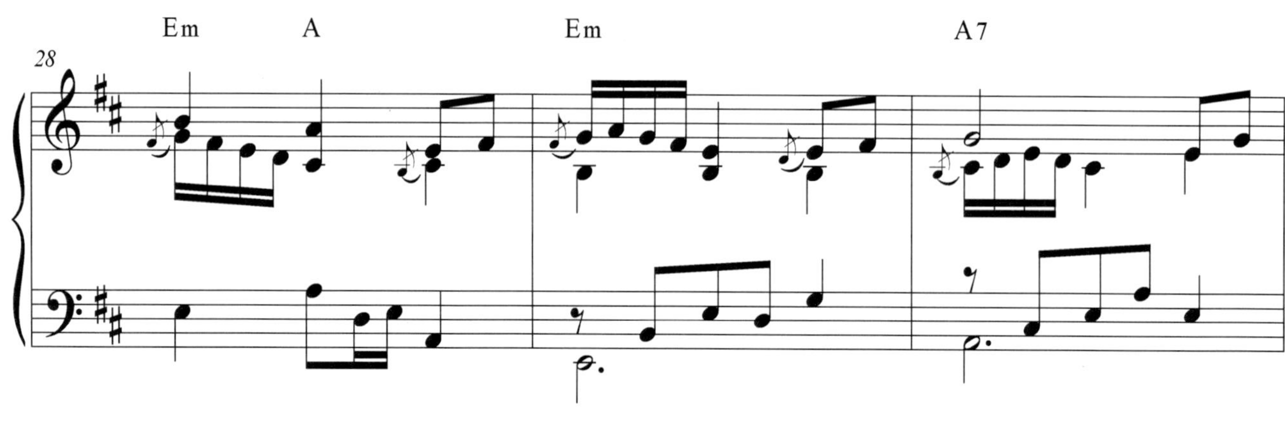
28
Em
A
Em
A7

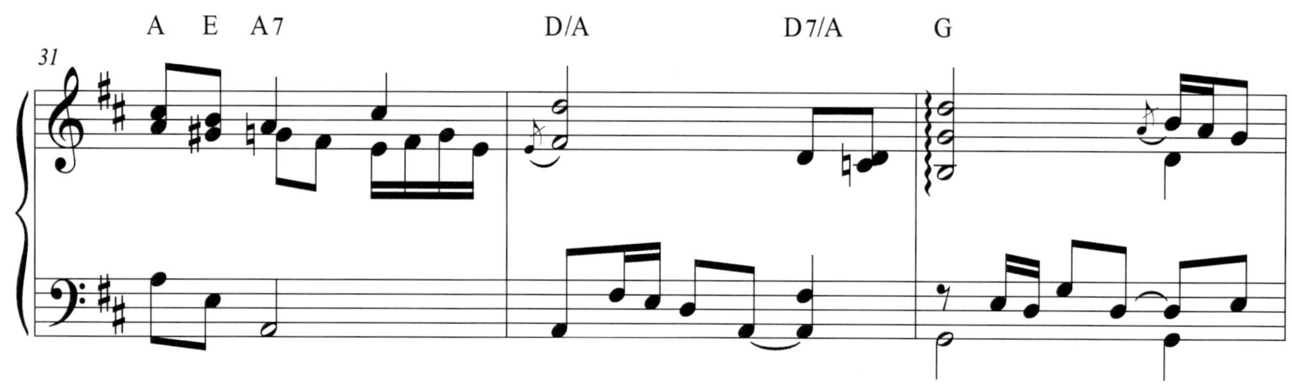
31
A
E
A7
D/A
D7/A
G

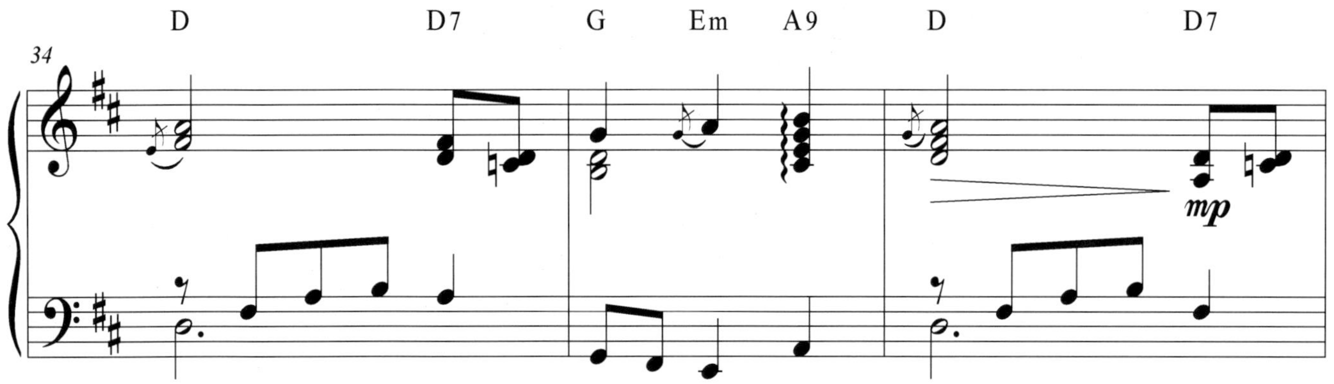
D
D7
G
Em
A9
D
D7
34
mp

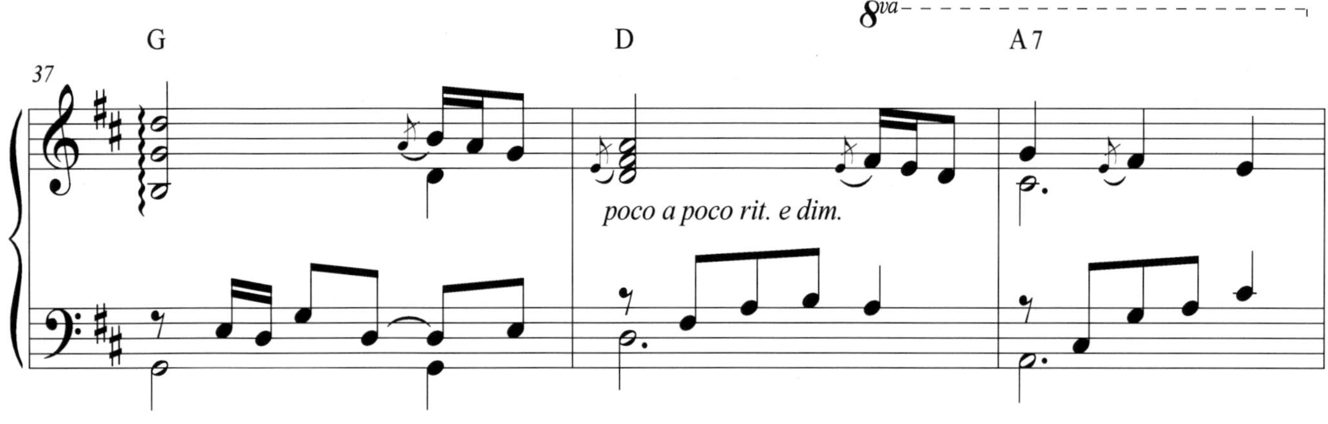
8va
G
D
A7
37
poco a poco rit. e dim.

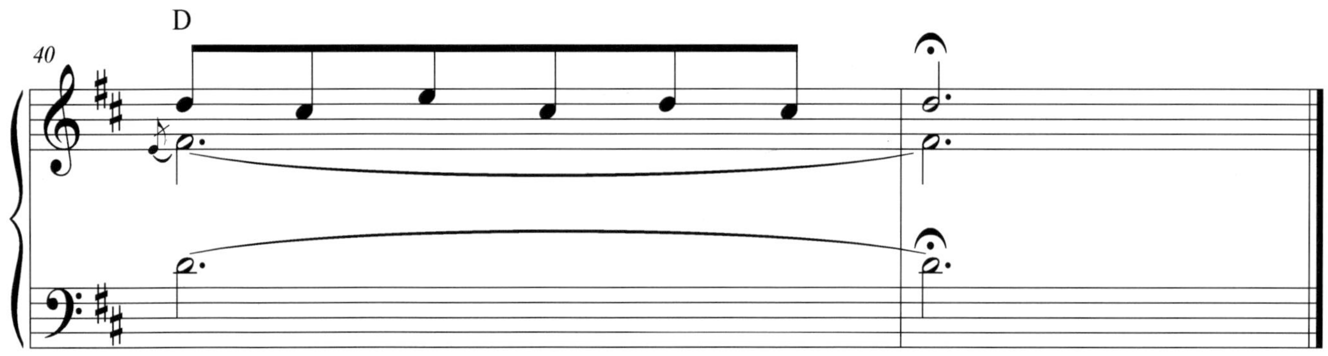
D
40

O Come, All Ye Faithful

7

Trans. by FREDERICK OAKELEY

JOHN F. WADE
Arr. Devan M. Archer

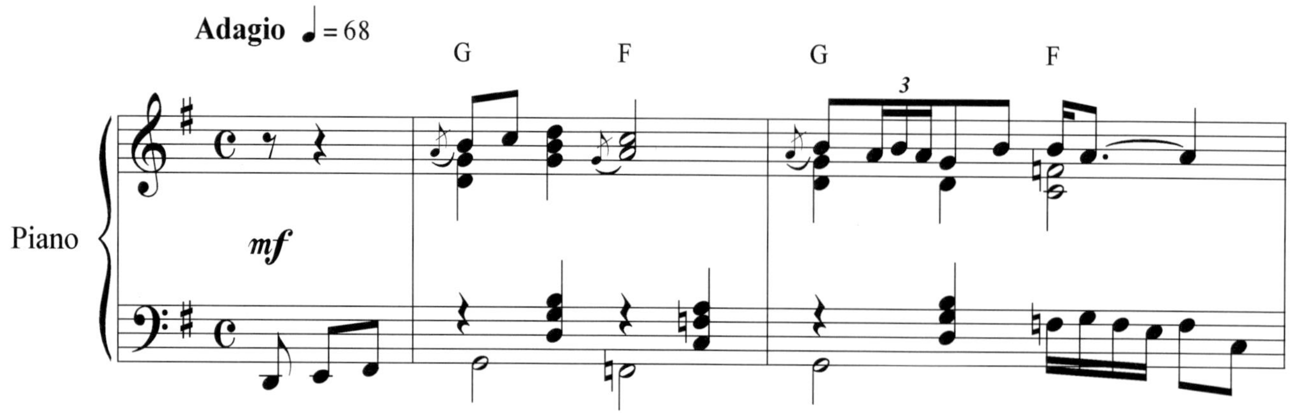

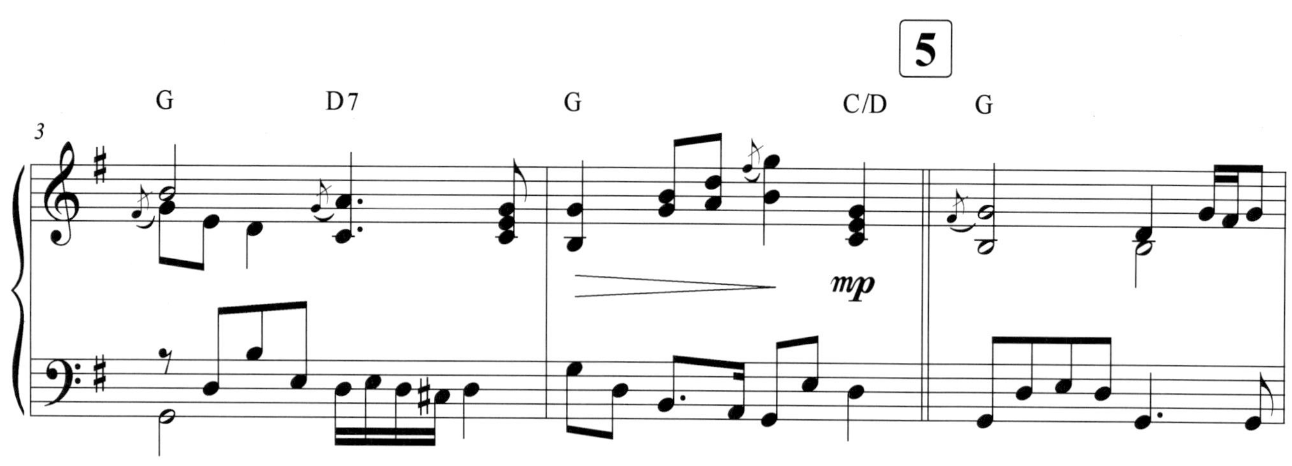

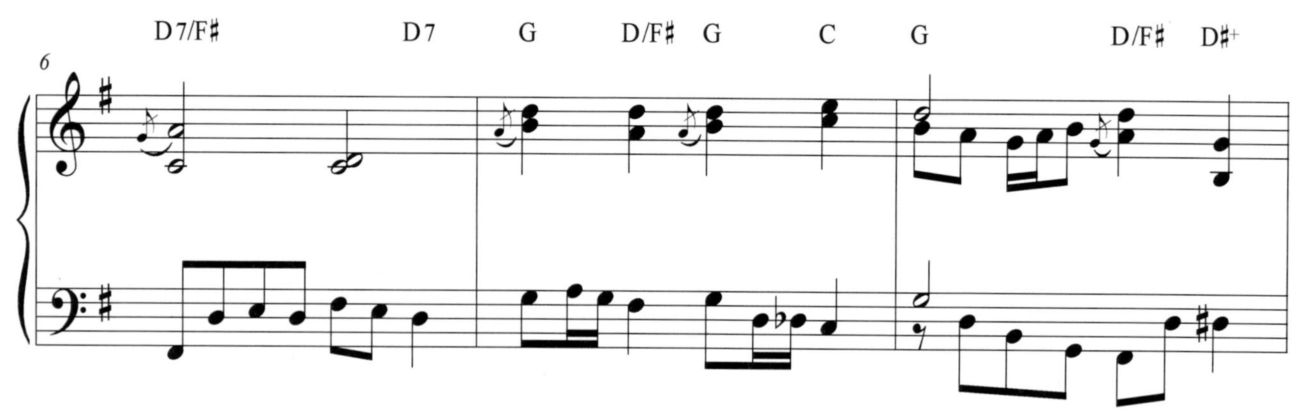

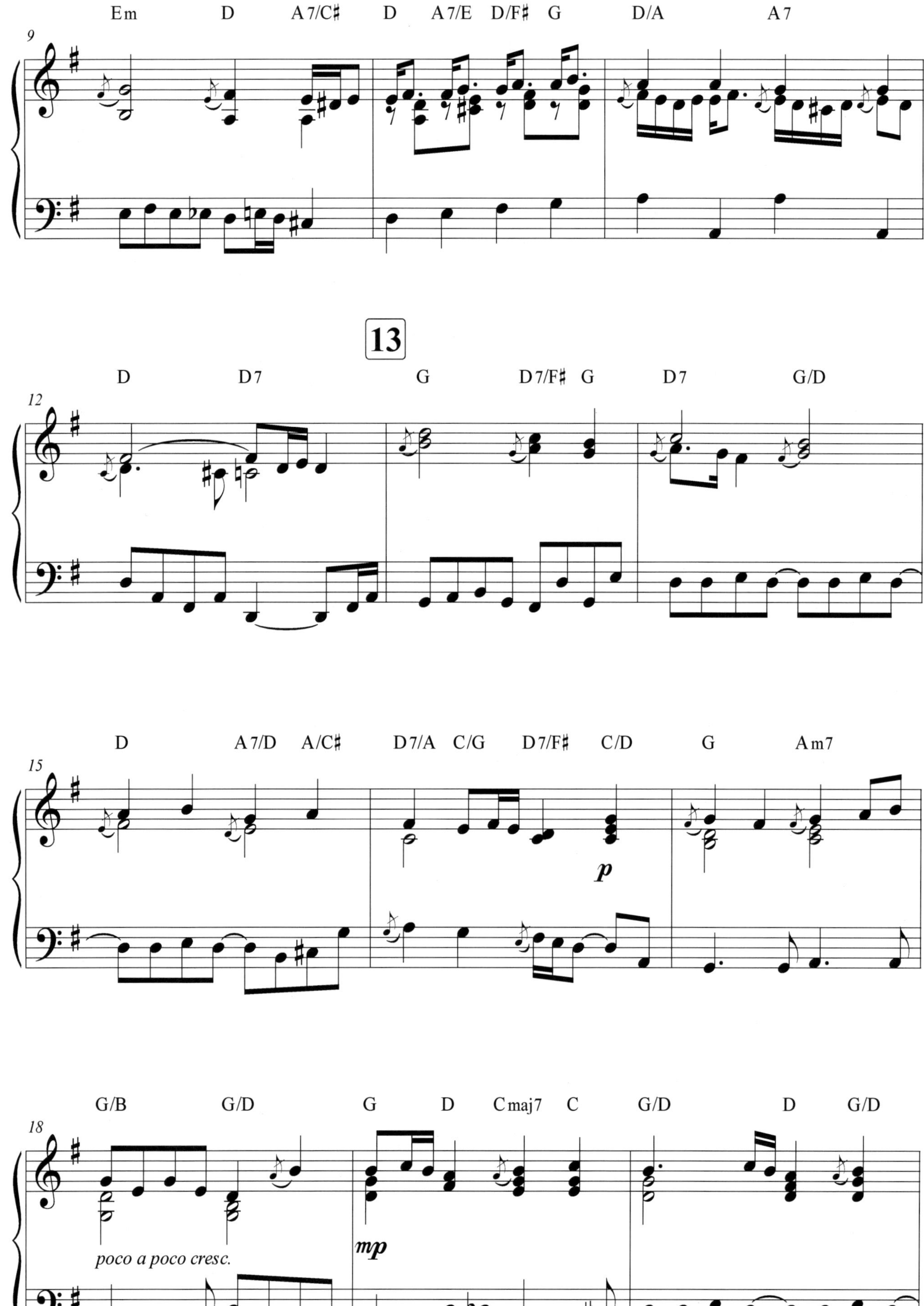
Em D A7/C♯ D A7/E D/F♯ G D/A A7
9
13
D D7 G D7/F♯ G D7 G/D
12
D A7/D A/C♯ D7/A C/G D7/F♯ C/D G Am7
15
p
G/B G/D G D Cmaj7 C G/D D G/D
18
poco a poco cresc.
mp

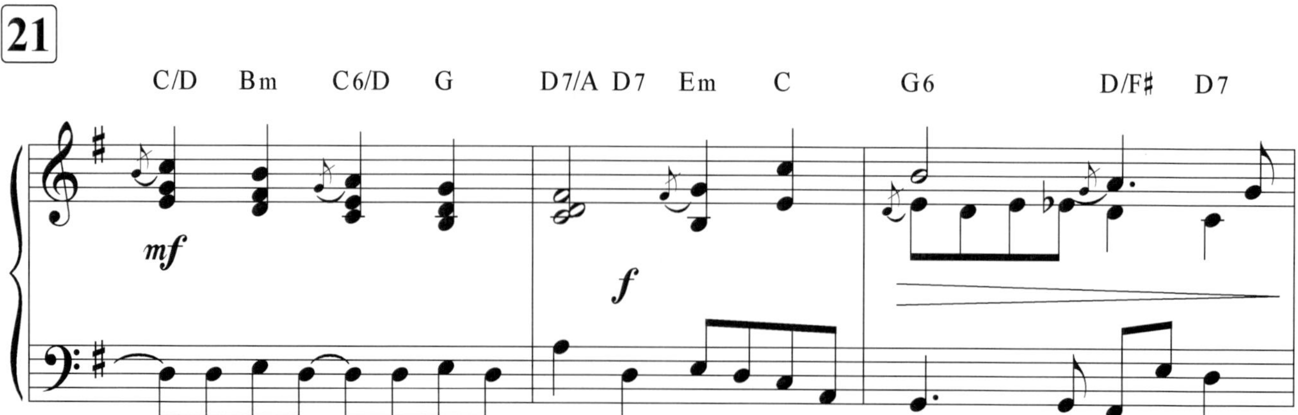
21
C/D Bm C6/D G D7/A D7 Em C G6 D/F♯ D7
mf
f

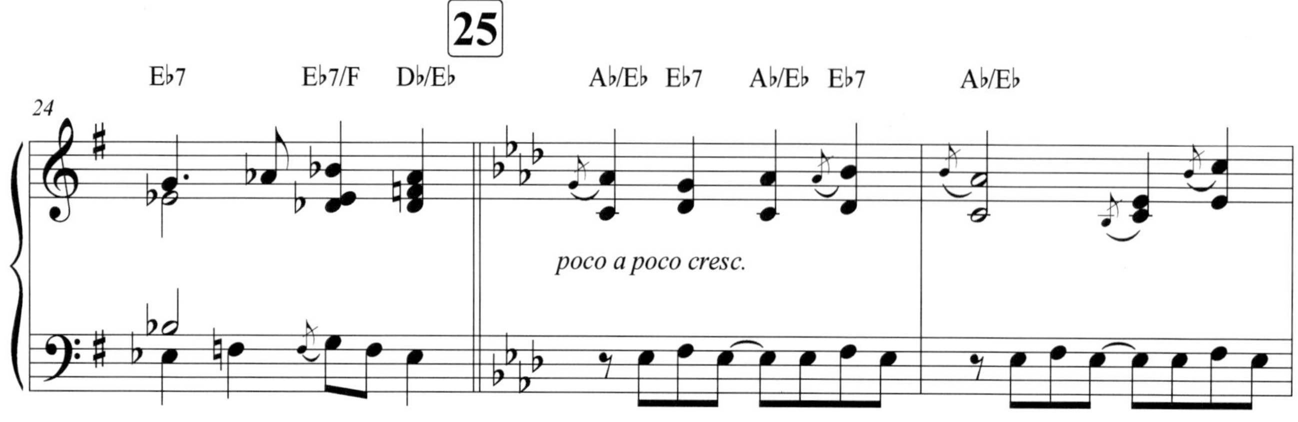
25
E♭7 E♭7/F D♭/E♭ A♭/E♭ E♭7 A♭/E♭ E♭7 A♭/E♭
24
poco a poco cresc.

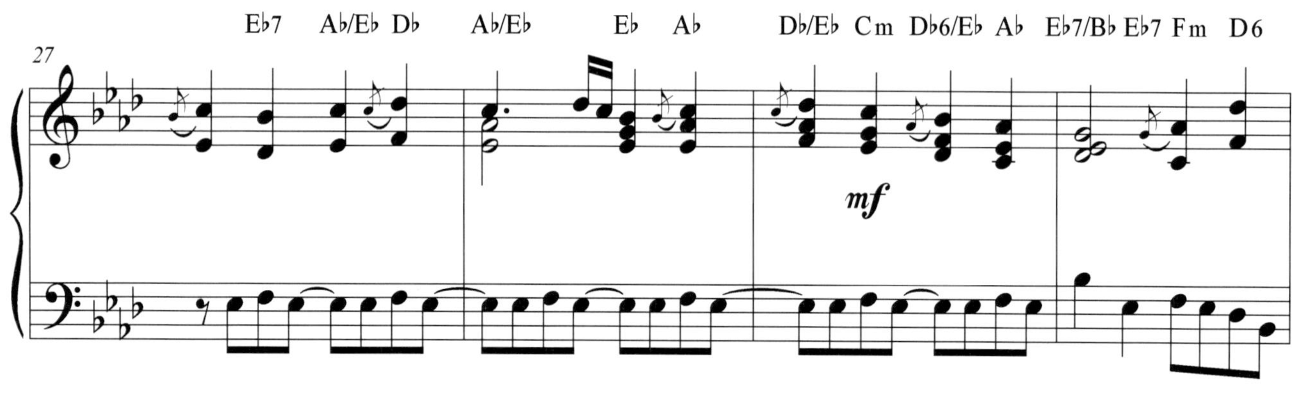
E♭7 A♭/E♭ D♭ A♭/E♭ E♭ A♭ D♭/E♭ Cm D♭6/E♭ A♭ E♭7/B♭ E♭7 Fm D6
27
mf

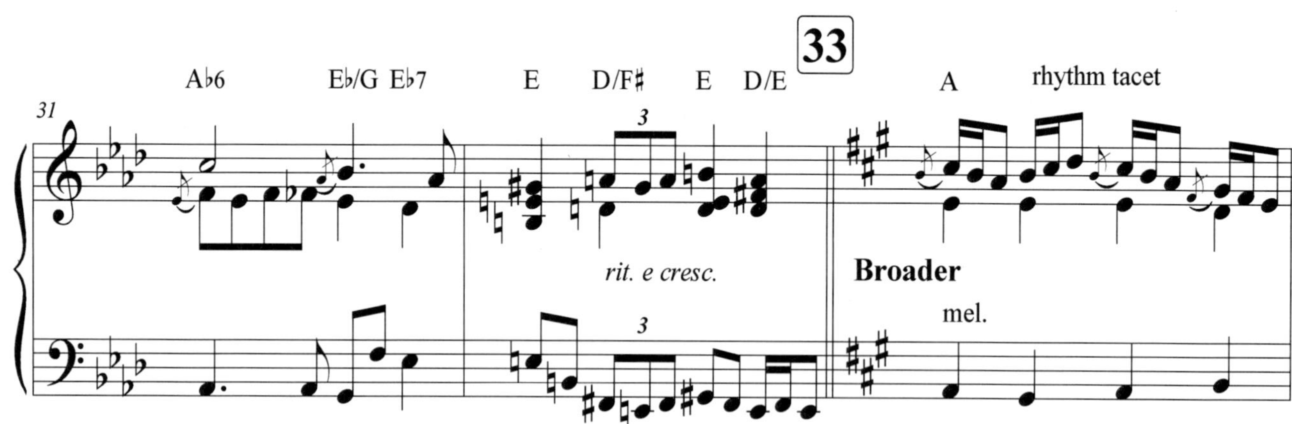
33
A♭6 E♭/G E♭7 E D/F♯ E D/E A rhythm tacet
31
3
rit. e cresc.
Broader
mel.

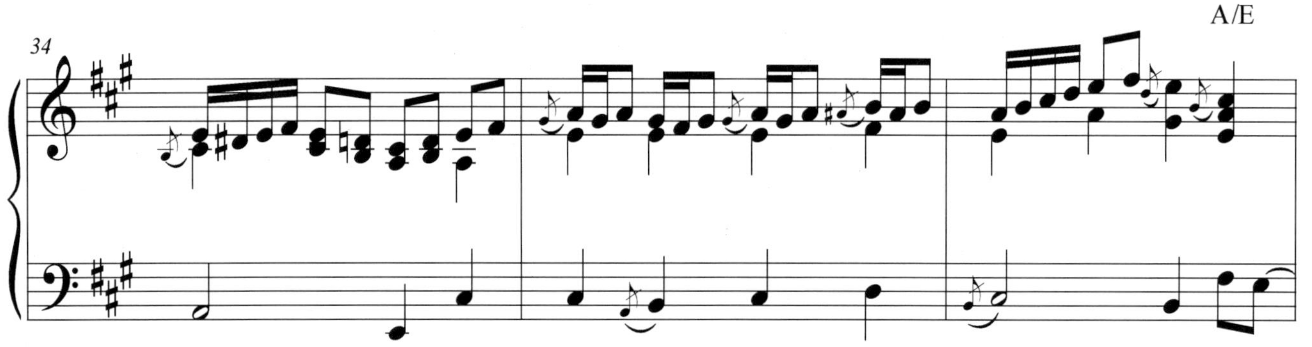
34
A/E

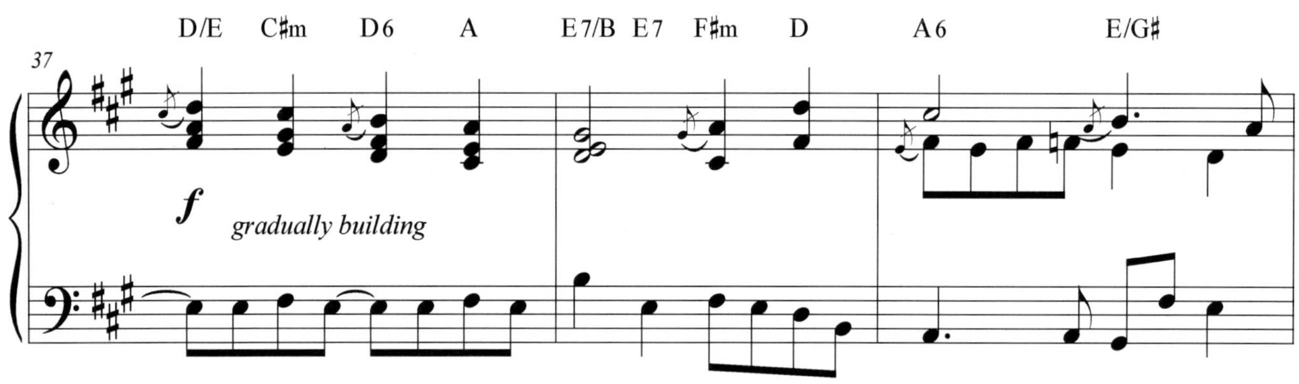
37
D/E
C♯m
D6
A
E7/B
E7
F♯m
D
A6
E/G♯
f
gradually building

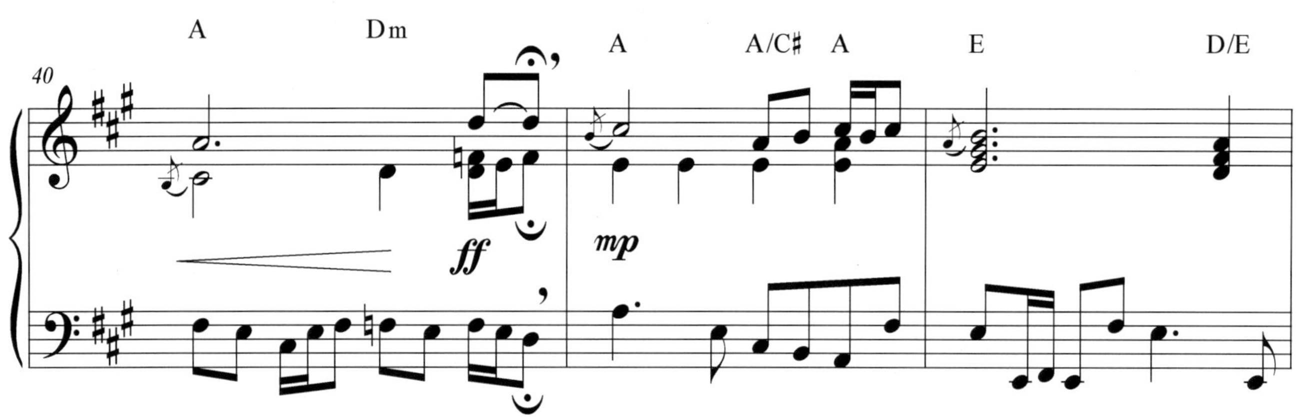
40
A
Dm
A
A/C♯
A
E
D/E
ff
mp

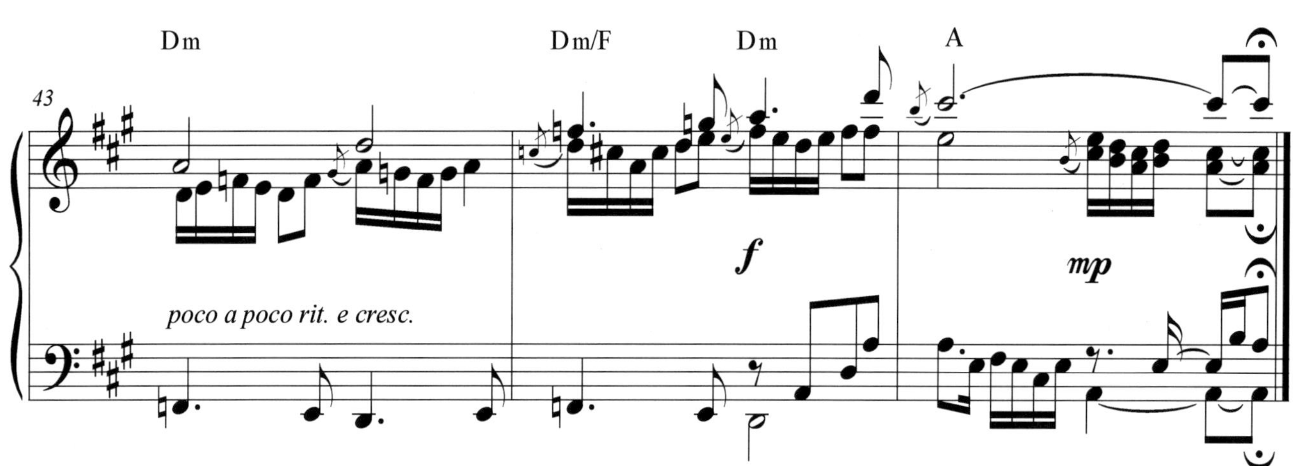
43
Dm
Dm/F
Dm
A
poco a poco rit. e cresc.
f
mp

Silent Night

JOSEPH MOHR

FRANZ GRUBER
Arr. Devan M. Archer

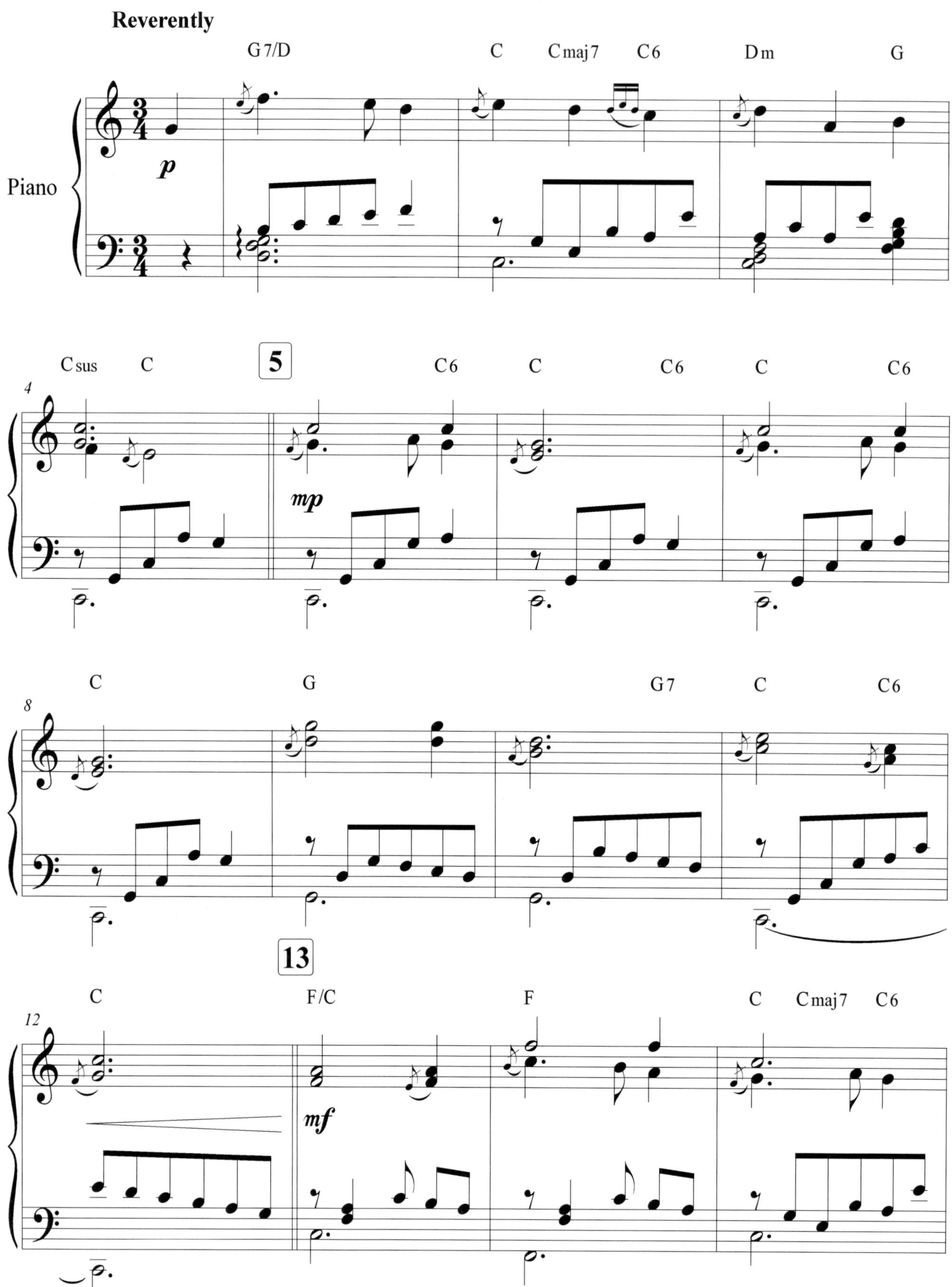

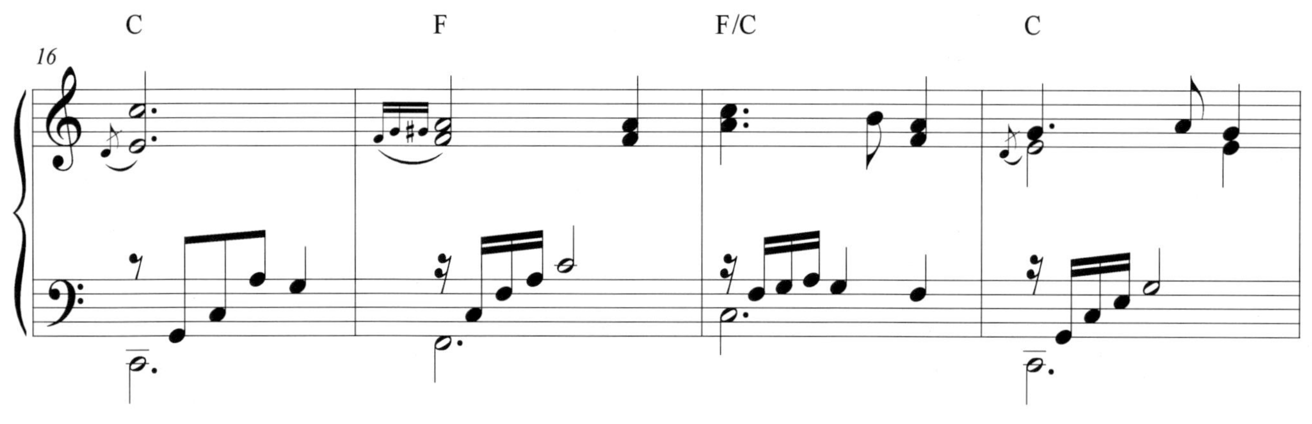
16
C
F
F/C
C

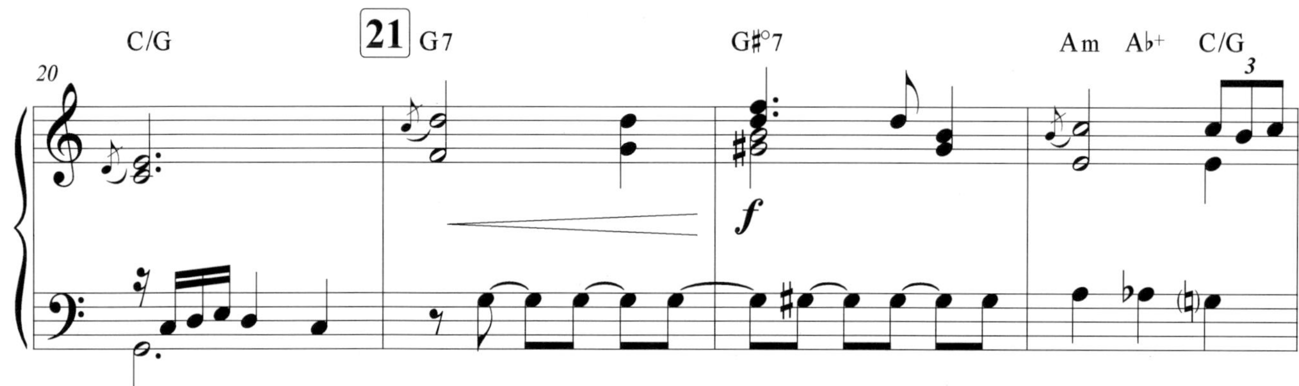
20
C/G
21
G7
G#°7
f
Am
A♭+
C/G
3

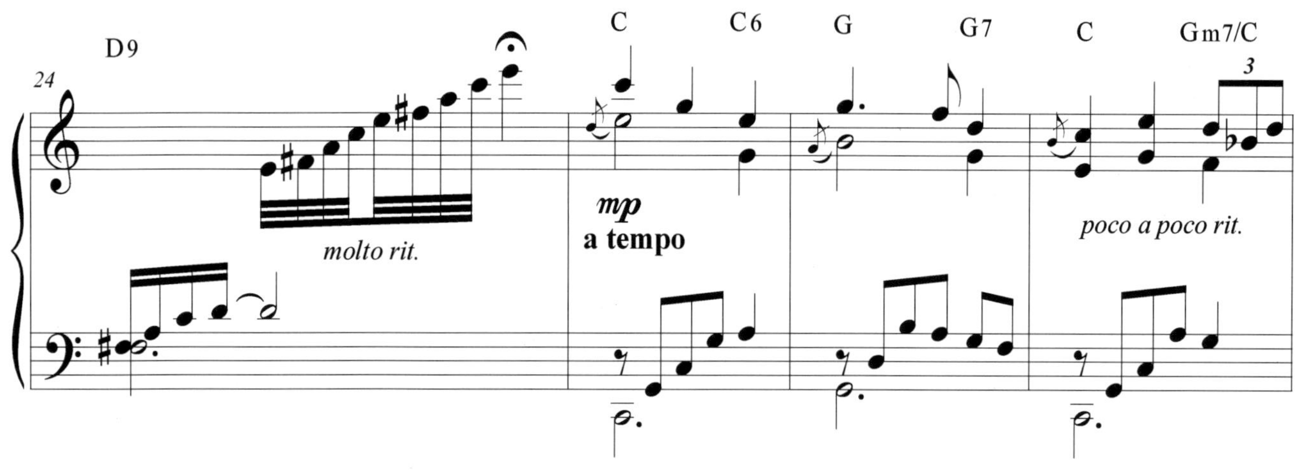
24
D9
molto rit.
C
C6
mp
a tempo
G
G7
C
Gm7/C
3
poco a poco rit.

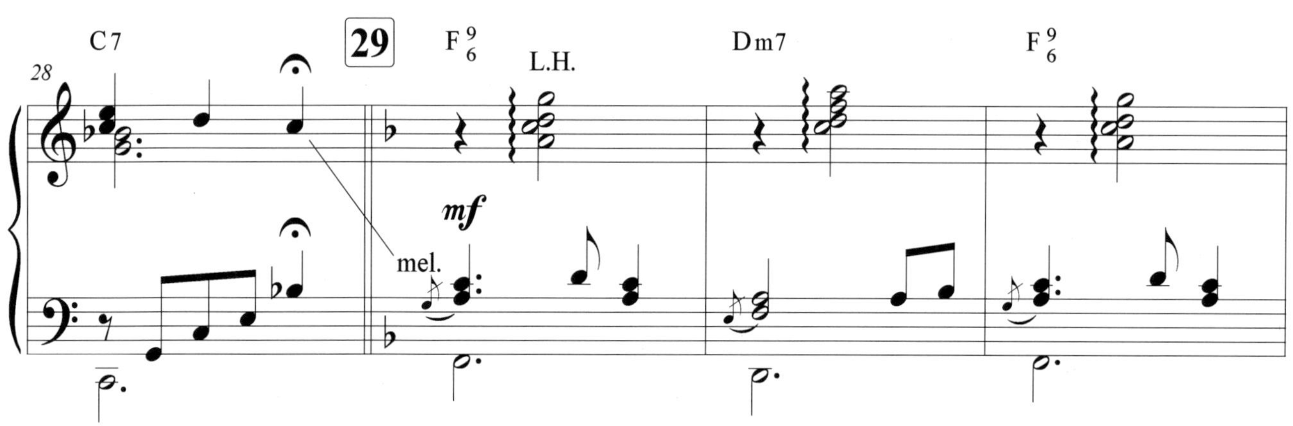
28
C7
29
F 9 6
L.H.
mf
mel.
Dm7
F 9 6

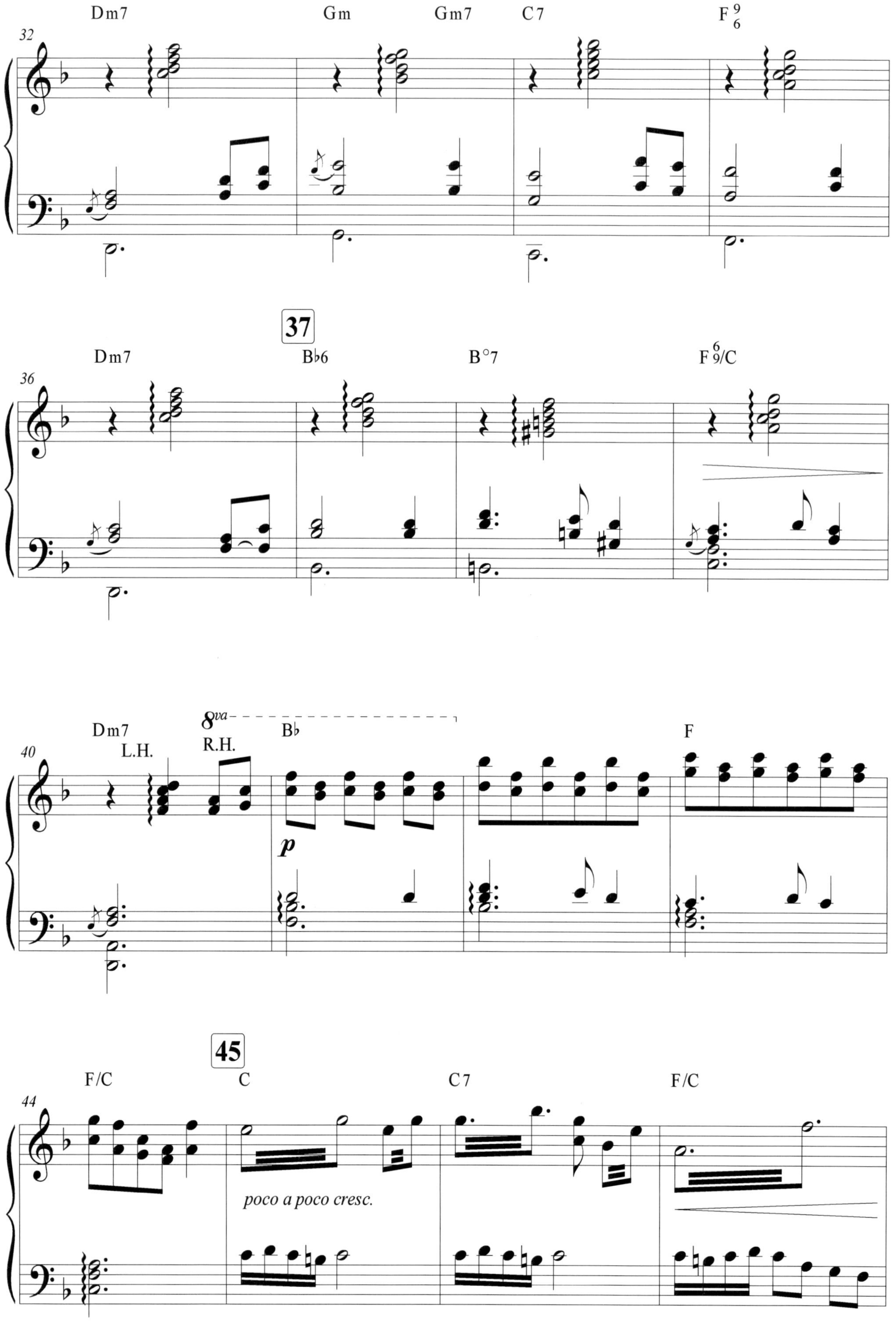

32
Dm7 Gm Gm7 C7 F 9 6

36
37
Dm7 B♭6 B°7 F 6 9/C

40
Dm7 8va B♭ F
L.H. R.H.
p

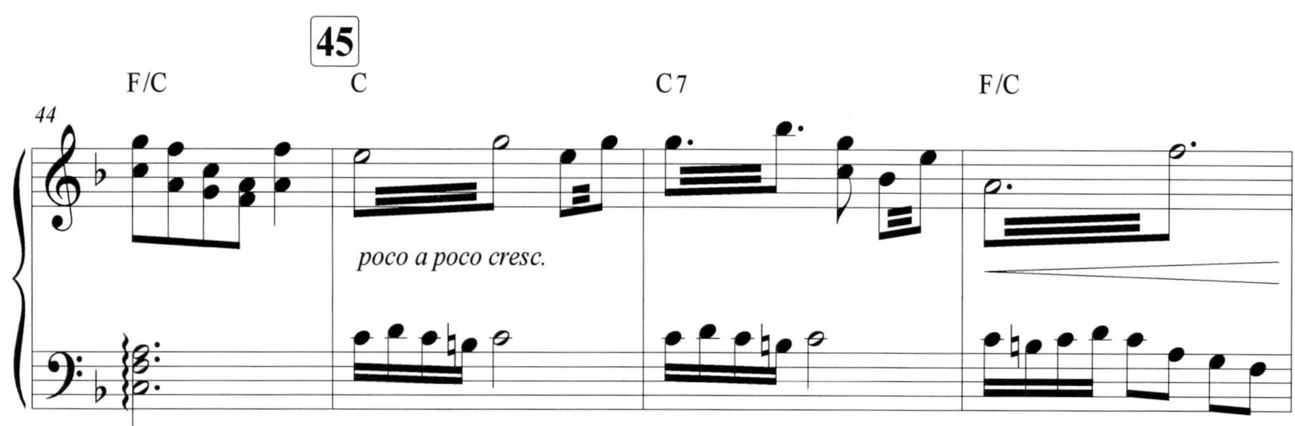

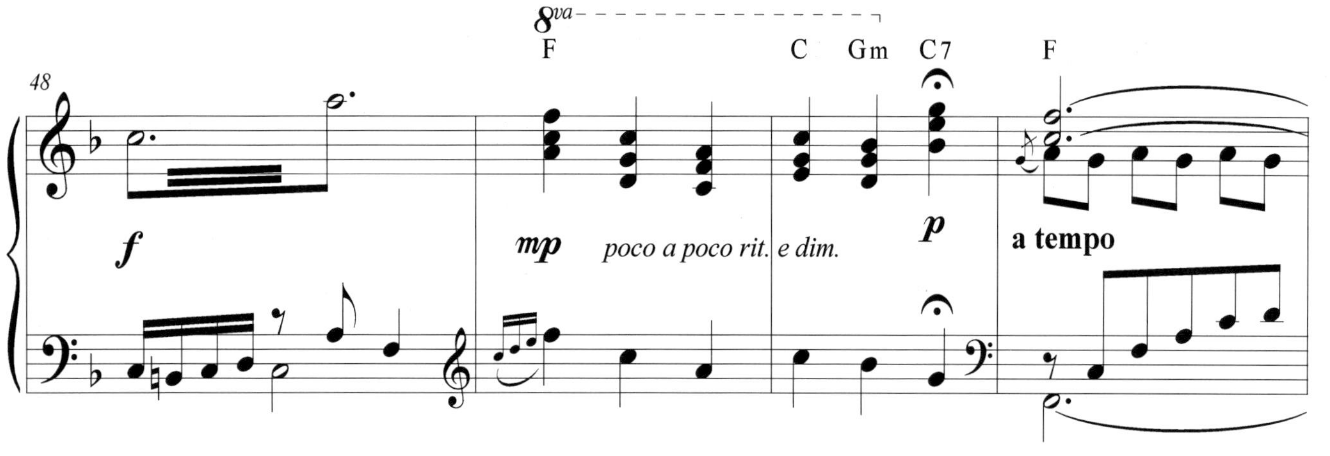
48
8va
F
C
Gm
C7
F
f
mp
poco a poco rit. e dim.
p
a tempo

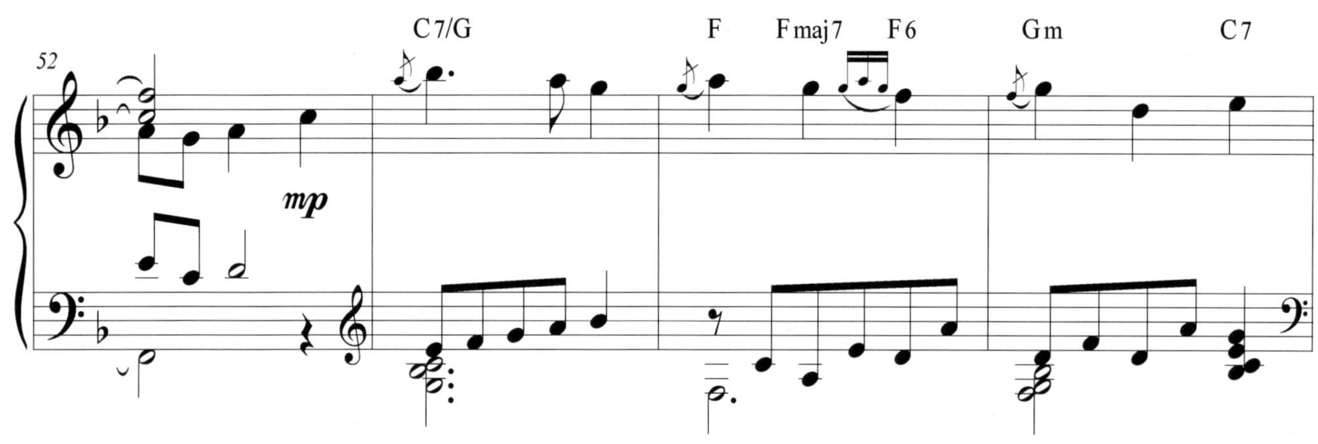
52
C7/G
F
Fmaj7
F6
Gm
C7
mp

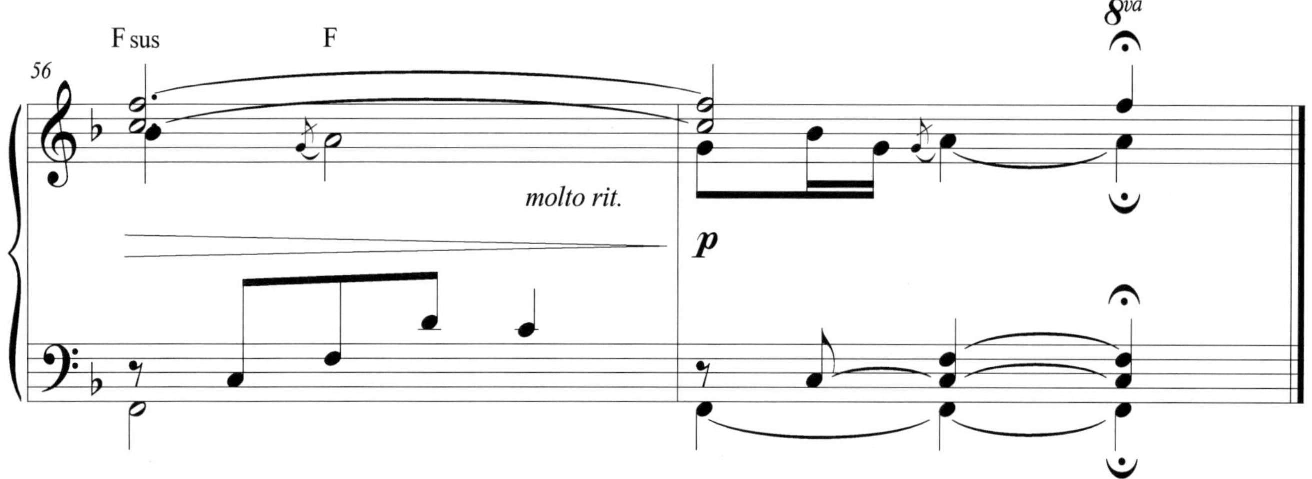
56
Fsus
F
8va
molto rit.
p

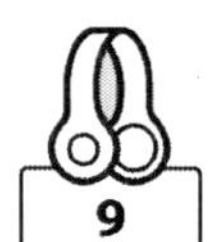

The First Noel

TRADITIONAL ENGLISH CAROL
Arr. Devan M. Archer

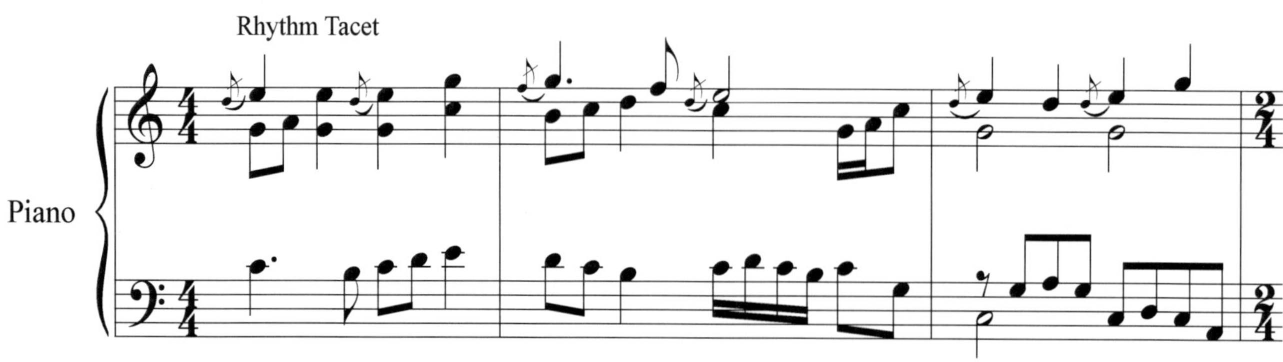

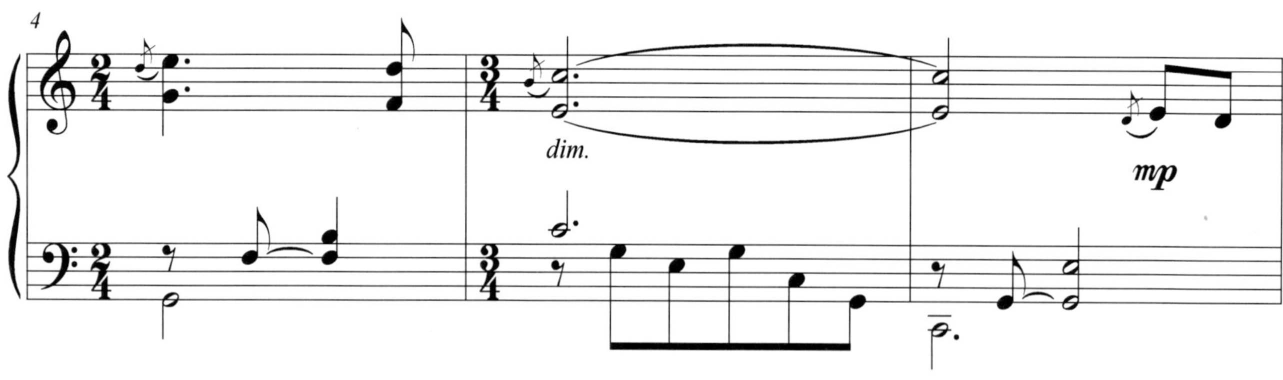

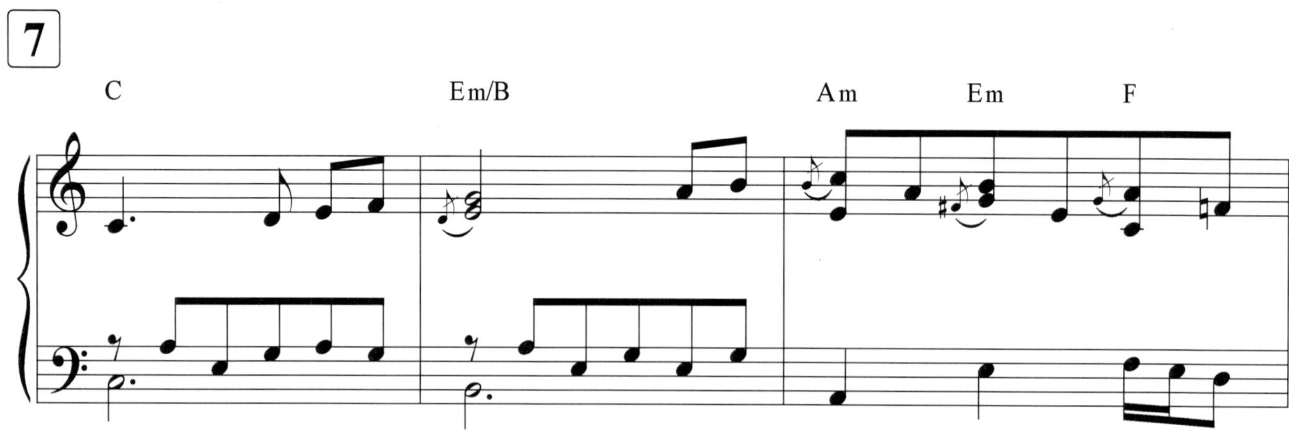

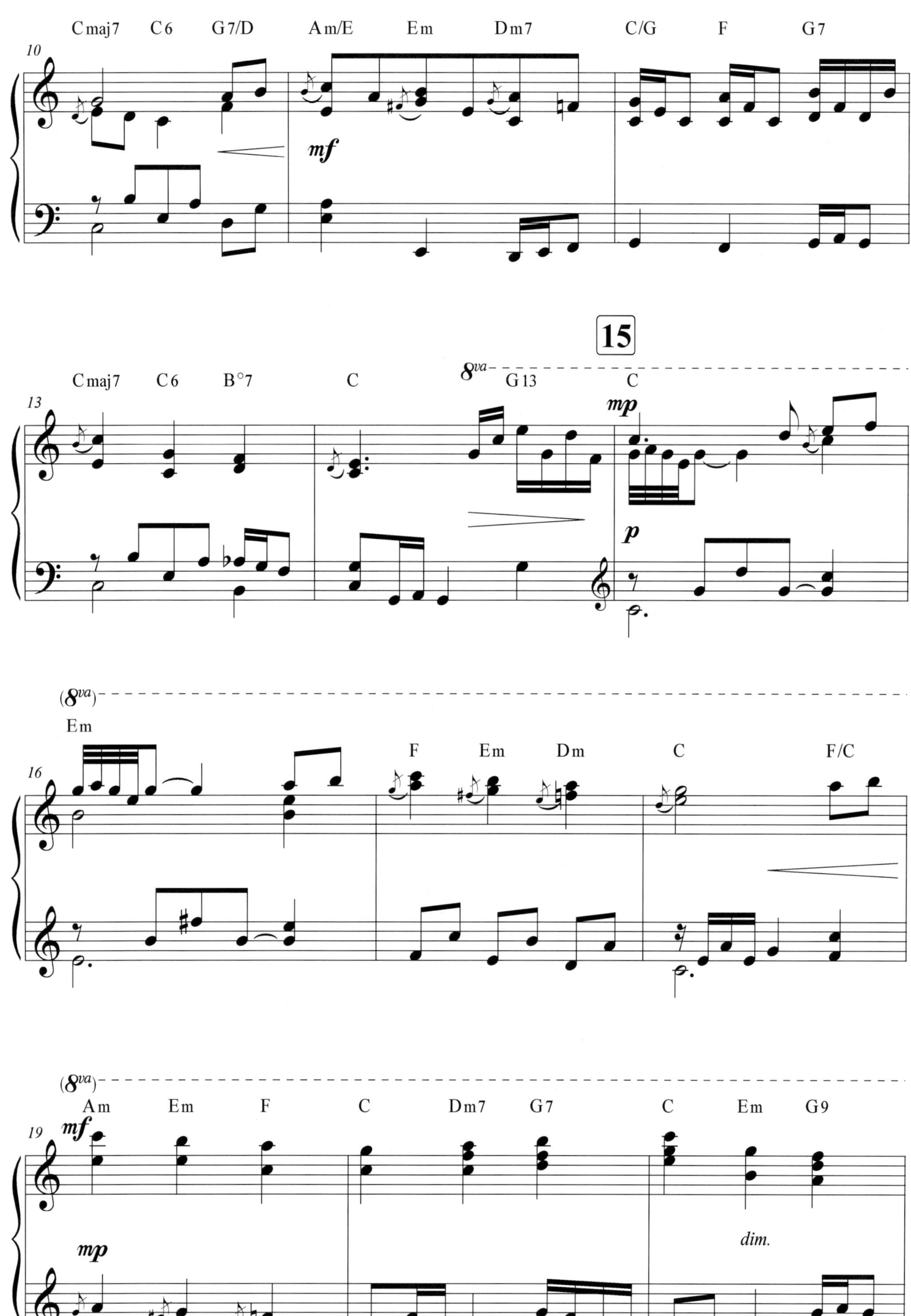
Cmaj7 C6 G7/D Am/E Em Dm7 C/G F G7
10
mf
15
8va
Cmaj7 C6 B°7 C G13 C
13
mp
p
(8va)
Em F Em Dm C F/C
16
(8va)
Am Em F C Dm7 G7 C Em G9
19
mf
mp
dim.

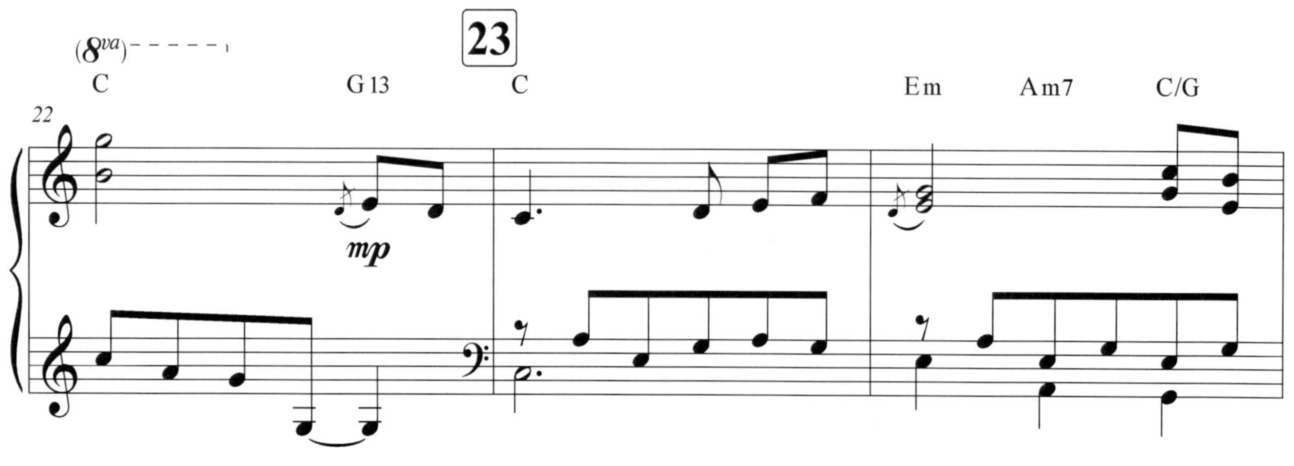
(8va)
23
C
G13
C
Em
Am7
C/G
22
mp

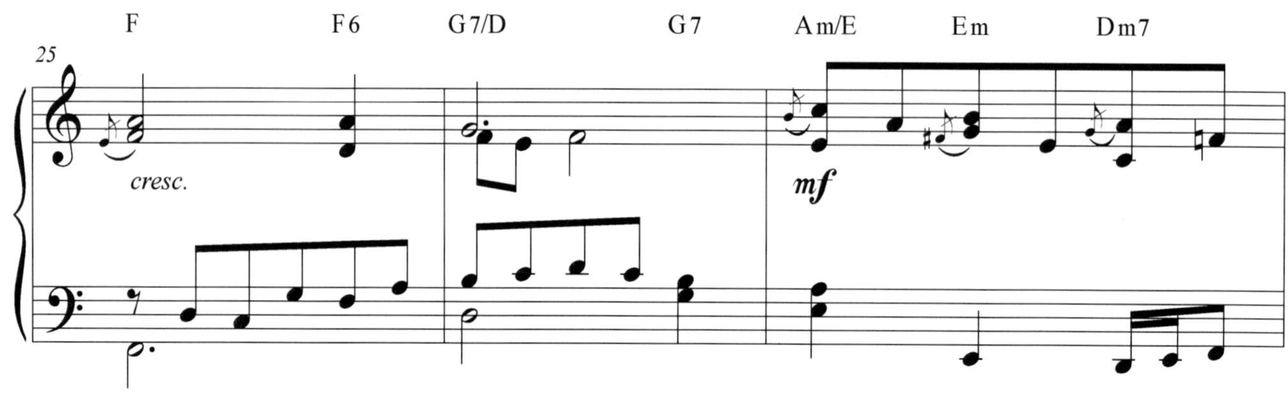
F
F6
G7/D
G7
Am/E
Em
Dm7
25
cresc.
mf

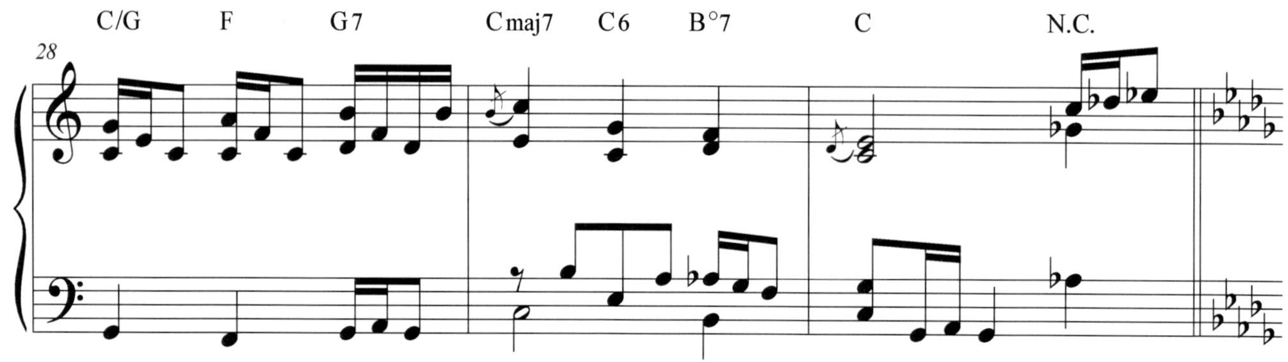
C/G
F
G7
Cmaj7
C6
B°7
C
N.C.
28

31

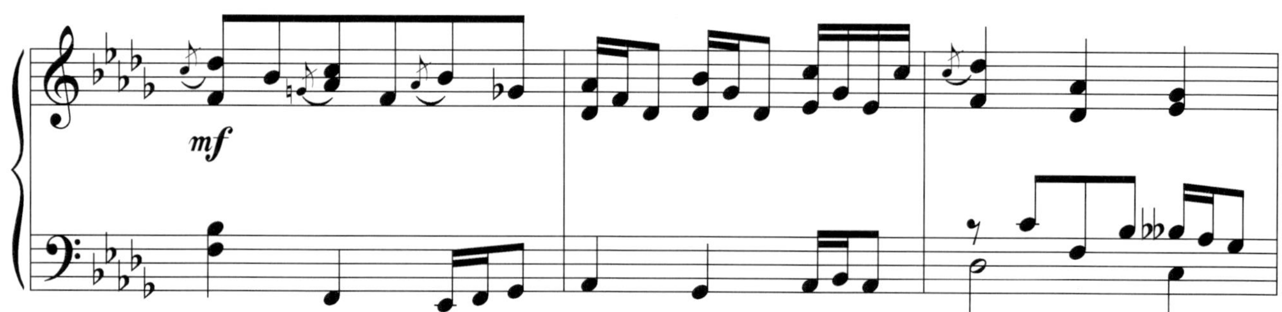
mf

34
D♭
F m
mel.

39

37
B♭m
F m
G♭
D♭
G♭
A♭/E♭
B♭m
F m
G♭
mel.

40
D♭
E♭m
A♭7
B♭m
D♭/F
A♭7
D♭
F♯m/A
A 7/C♯
mel.

43
D
F♯m
B m
F♯m
G
mf
f

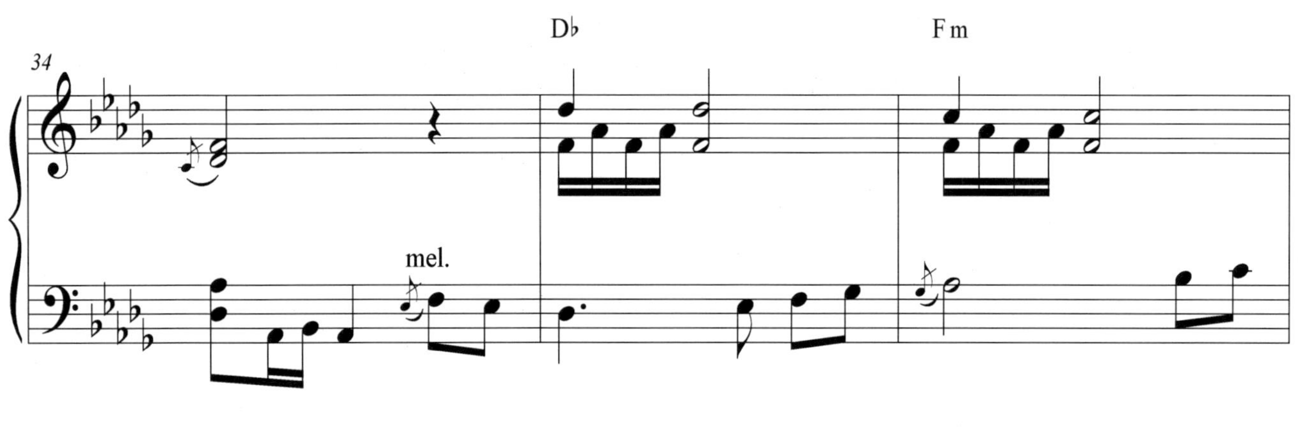

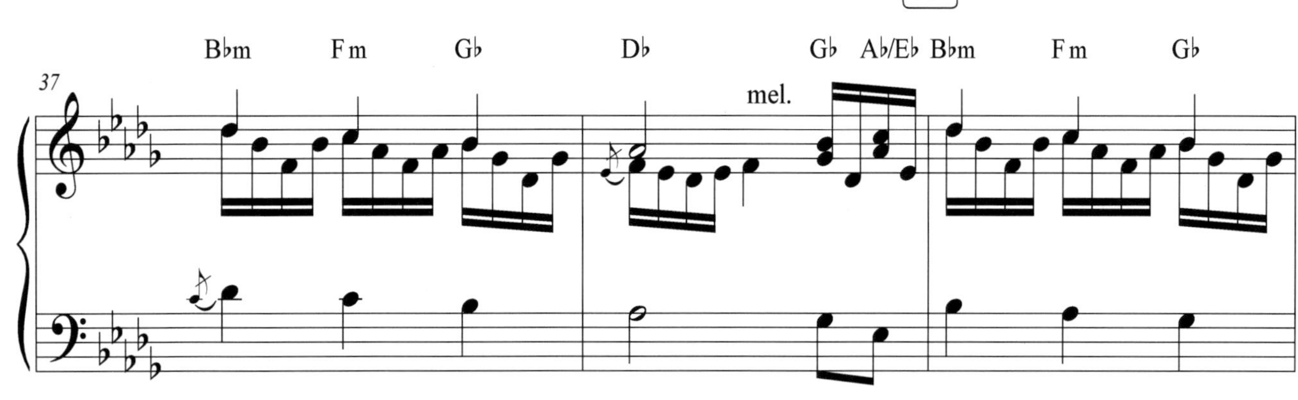

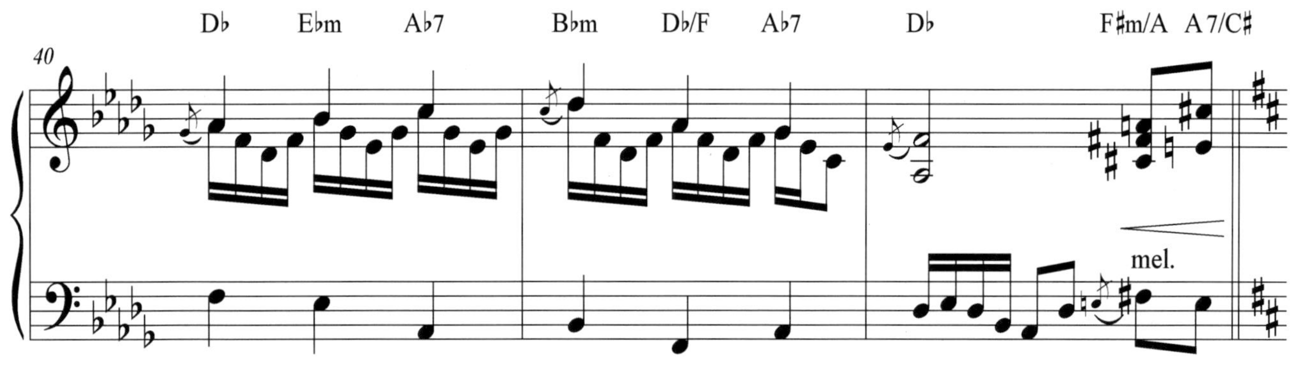

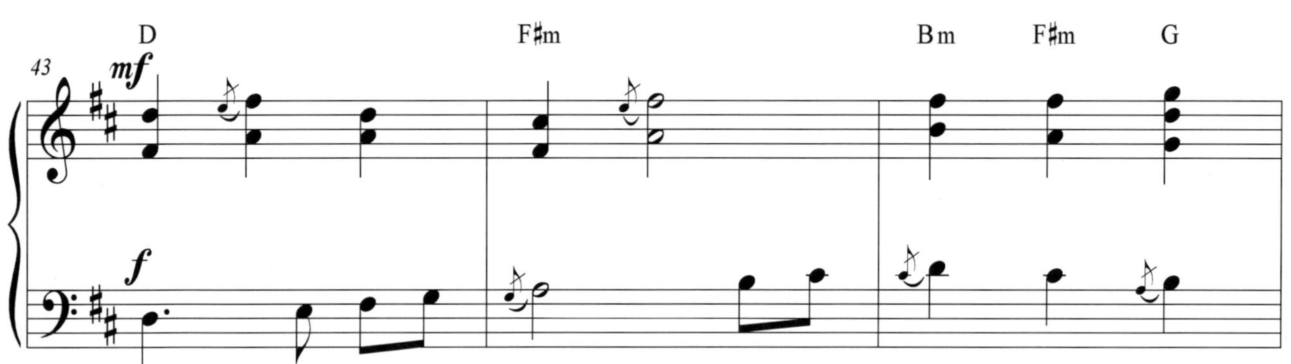

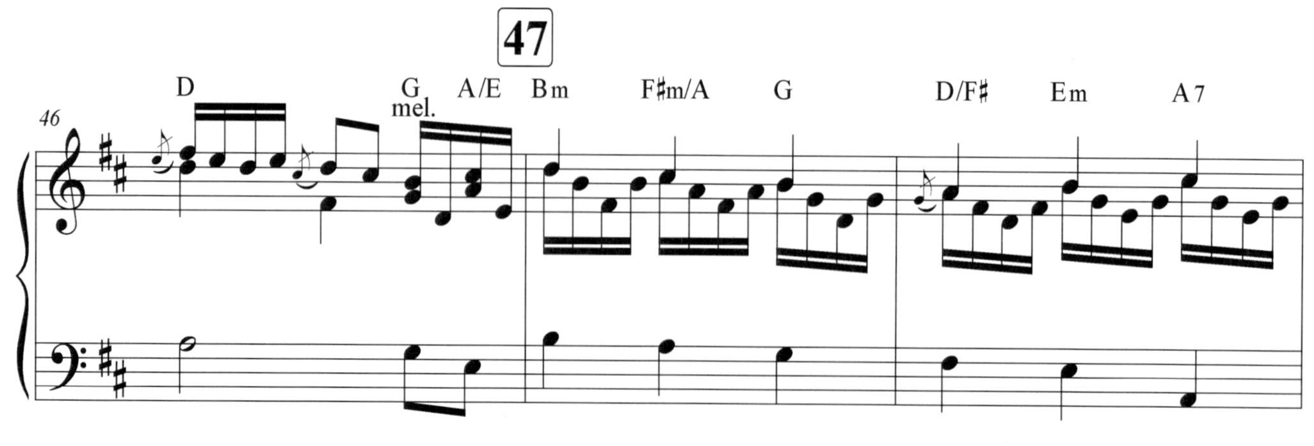
47
D
G
mel.
A/E
Bm
F♯m/A
G
D/F♯
Em
A7
46

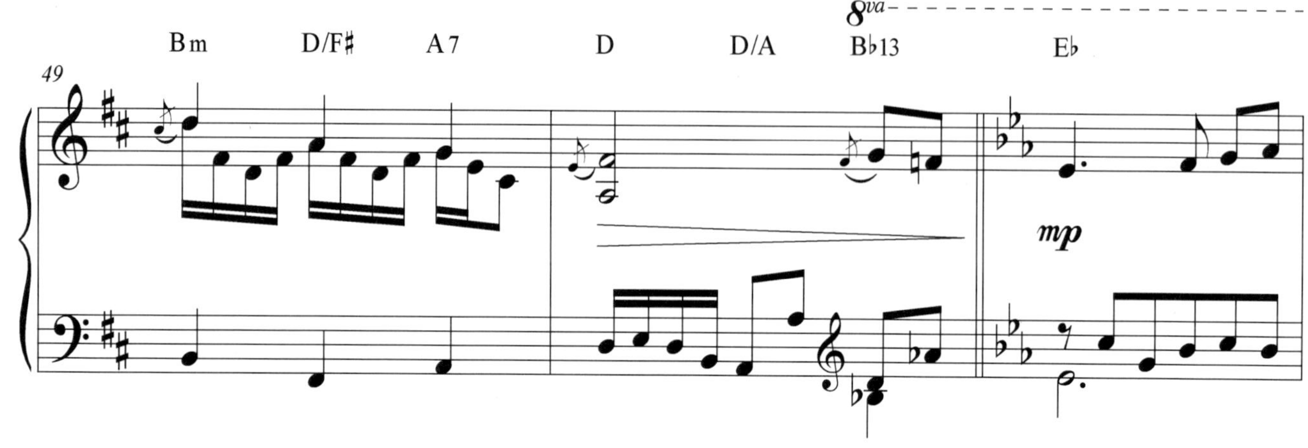
8va
Bm
D/F♯
A7
D
D/A
B♭13
E♭
49
mp

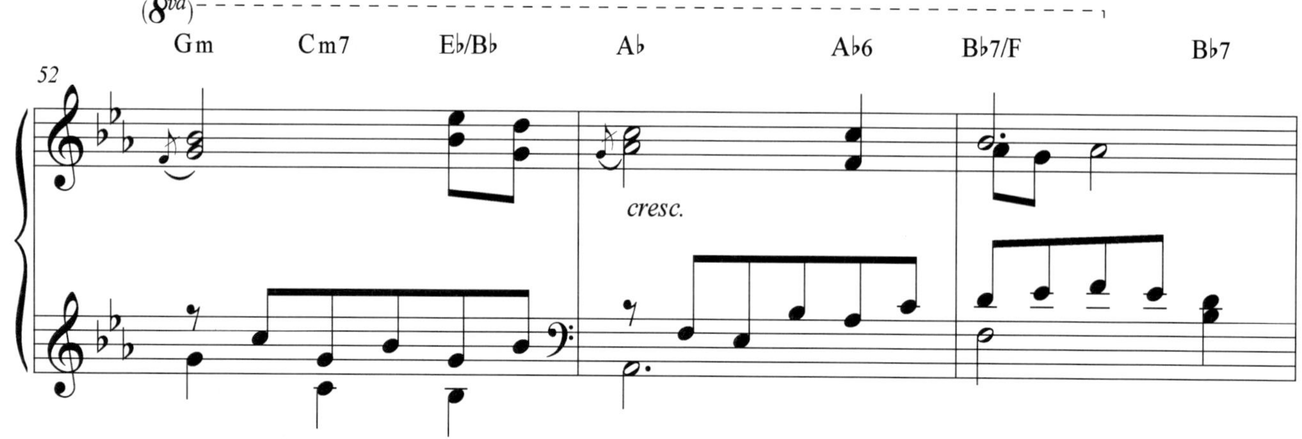
(8va)
Gm
Cm7
E♭/B♭
A♭
A♭6
B♭7/F
B♭7
52
cresc.

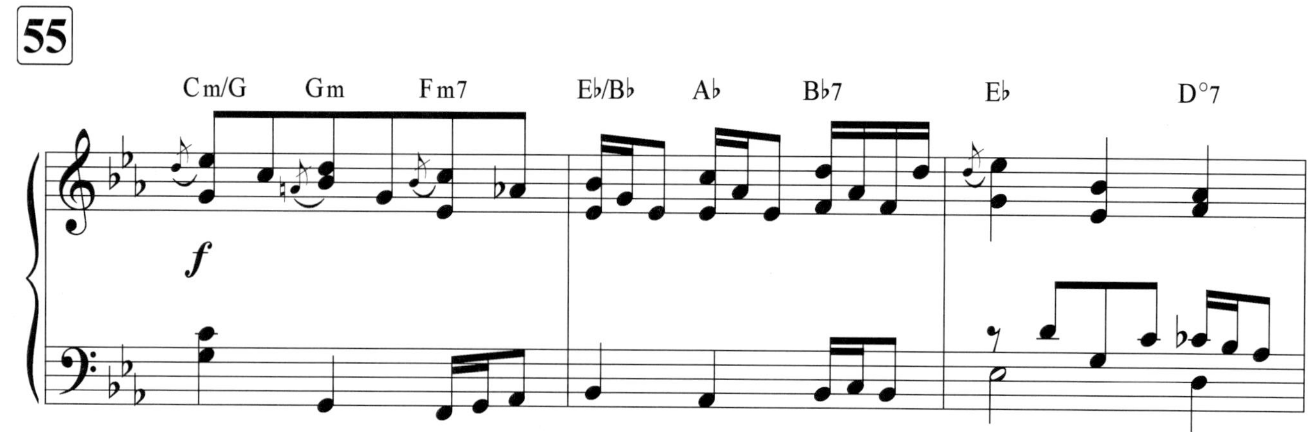
55
Cm/G
Gm
Fm7
E♭/B♭
A♭
B♭7
E♭
D°7
f

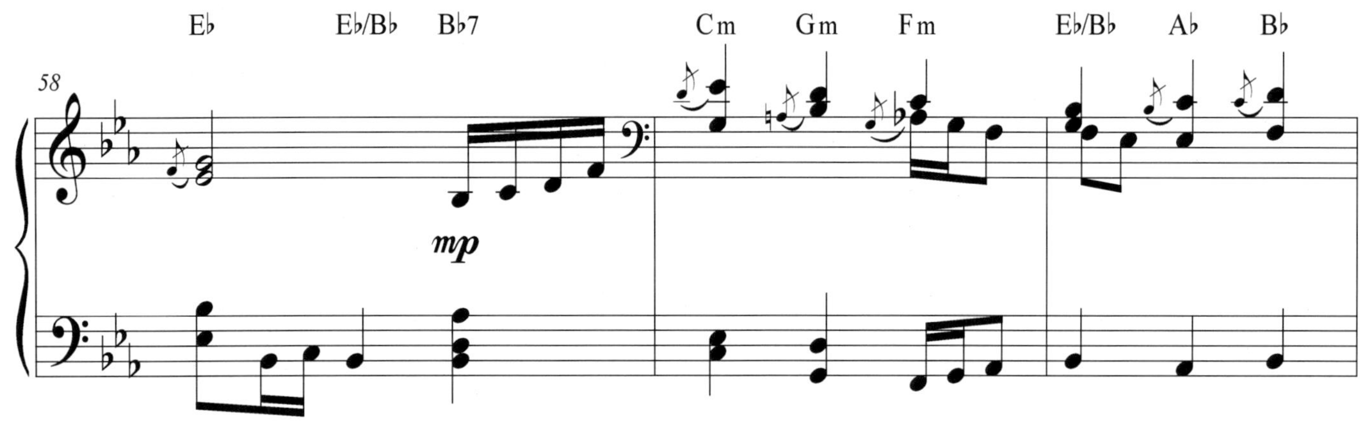
E♭
E♭/B♭
B♭7
C m
G m
F m
E♭/B♭
A♭
B♭
58
mp

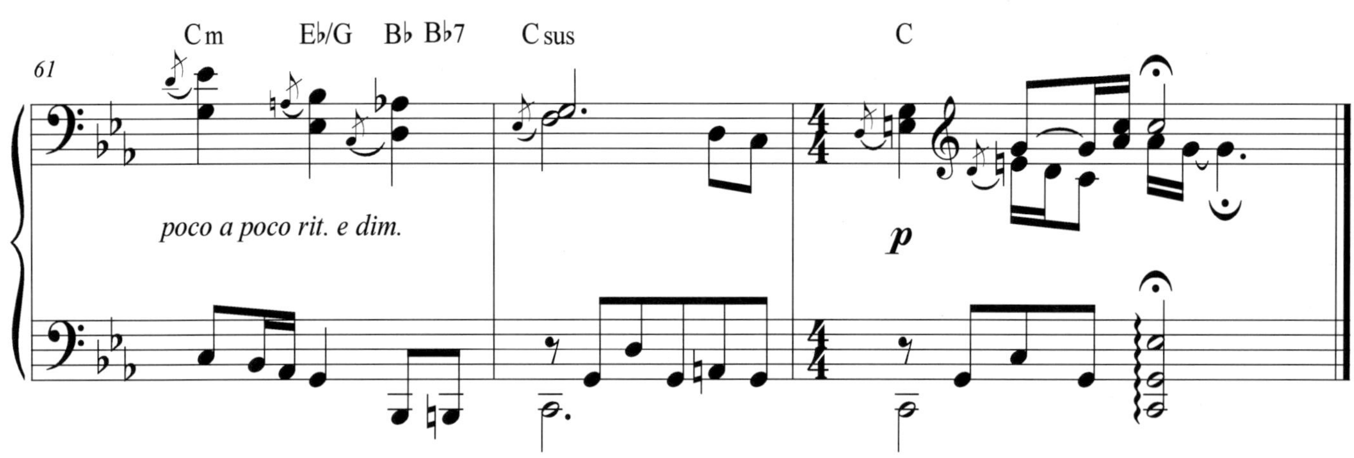
C m
E♭/G
B♭
B♭7
C sus
C
61
poco a poco rit. e dim.
p

Other Mel Bay Piano Books